The Glorious Destiny of Israel

גור גוררלה המפואר של ישראל

The Fulfillment of G-d's Promises and Prophecies to Israel

התגשמות ההבטחות והנבואות של אלוהים לישראל

SECOND EDITION

Dr. David Alan Greene

GraceWord Publishing, LLC
www.gracewordpublishing.com
U.S.A.

GRACEWORD PUBLISHING

Contents

To The Sons and Daughters of Abraham

For I know the thoughts that I think toward you,
saith the LORD, thoughts of peace, and not of evil,
to give you <u>a future and a hope</u>.

- Jeremiah 29.11

x

Acknowledgements

I would like to express my gratitude to GraceWord Publishing who agreed to publish this book. I am grateful to them for their continued support and the volunteers who helped with the preparation of this book.

Preface

My background is somewhat unique when compared to other theologians, those studying G-d. For I am neither a pastor nor am I affiliated with any sectarian group. Therefore, I am independent in my approach. I will not suggest you join any group, make any donation, or do anything. I am not trying to change your theological beliefs. Only you, as an individual, can do that. You decide what you will believe and reject as truth. All I ask is that you sit back with an open mind and consider what I am presenting. As you read this book, please think about the ideas and evidence presented. This would especially apply if it is not something you have heard before. Most likely, it is something you are just seeing from a different perspective.

For years, I was a property and casualty insurance agent. In the field of insurance, everything centers around one document – the insurance policy. I believe that formed the basis of my approach to Scripture. Once someone buys a policy (home, auto, boat, etc.) and they have a claim, the policy coverage is determined by the coverage in effect at the time of the loss. Similarly, what someone has chosen to believe or reject as truth is sealed at death and, according to Scripture, what someone has chosen to believe determines their eternal destiny. There will be no second chance. There are no do-overs. Like a policy, Scripture says what it says whether we agree with it or not, whether we read it or not; whether we believe it or not. Therefore, the eternal destiny of all people, whether Jew or non-Jew, will be determined by what was written in Scripture.

In this book, you will find that all quotes from the Law, the Writings, and the Prophets were taken from the JPS Tanakh 1917. This is considered by many to be the most conservative. Any quotes from the New Testament will be from the King James Version also considered by many to be the most conservative. If you choose to use another version, this may have an effect on your following along. Also, within some of the verses, I have included underlining and bracketed comments where I feel it may be beneficial to the reader. This is not intended to alter the original text, but only to clarify it.

Many people fear Scripture because of what it may say. Some feel it is too cumbersome or too much work to read and understand. Others view it as outdated and, therefore, no longer applicable today. I believe that it was the intention of the Author to reveal Himself and His plans in a way that can be understood by those willing to invest their time to read it. This book will cover the content of both the Old Covenant and New Covenant. You will see that these two are seamlessly joined together in both their theme and their message. There is wonderful news for the sons and daughters of Abraham!

Those who chose to ignore its contents, do so at their own peril. The confidence one has in their future and ultimate destiny is based upon their belief system. That system of belief is called "faith." What exactly is *faith?* Think of Abraham as you read the following definition. Hebrews 11.1:

> 1 **Now faith is the substance of things hoped for, the evidence of things not seen.**

The foundation of faith must be built upon unchangeable truth which is also called :absolute truth." There is only one source of unchangeable truth and that is the Word of G-d recorded for us in Scripture. What may surprise you is that this recorded truth was entrusted by G-d to a select group of people chosen for that specific purpose. I say this to both Jew, but especially the non-Jew. All people who read and trust Scripture are indebted to the Jews. For, without them, there would be no trustworthy record of the oracles of G-d. The Apostle Paul who is called the Apostle to the Gentiles agreed. He was a Pharisee who studied at the feet of Gamaliel. He instructed the Gentiles of this important of the Jews. Romans 3.1-2:

> 1 **What advantage then hath the Jew? or what profit is there of circumcision?**

> 2 **Much [in] every way: chiefly, because that unto them were committed the oracles of G-d.**

It began with Moses who received the first five books of the Old Covenant, The Torah, directly from G-d. This was followed by the Writings and the Prophets. They were written down and meticulously preserved by the Jews. What about the books the Christians call the New Testament? They too were written by Jews! Some believe that Luke was a Gentile because he was referred to as "Grecian." This is a common mistake. It would be similar to saying that an American or Canadian Jew is not a Jew. Luke, the author of the gospel of Luke and the book The Acts, was a Jew from Grecia. Like many from the Diaspora, they lived in different countries until they are called to return.

Going forward, I think it is important to point out an important fact. This book is dedicated to and written for the benefit of the sons and daughters of Abraham – the Jews! It is not being written for Christians, although they are more than welcome to learn about Israel's glorious destiny. Many evangelical Christians have a great affinity for Israel and, if they do not, they should. This book is specifically written to the sons and daughters of Abraham. They are a unique group of people chosen by G-d. That is not just my opinion. G-d wrote about them in Deuteronomy 14.2:

> 2 **For thou [Israel] art a holy people unto the LORD thy G-d, and the LORD hath chosen thee to be His own treasure out of all peoples that are upon the face of the earth.**

In the above verse it is important to see the word *holy* which means "separate." It does not mean perfect. In other words, Israel was separated by G-d from all the other nations.

When I use the name Israel, I am not writing about a geopolitical entity. I write about one family. I am writing about the sons and daughters of Abraham, Isaac, and Jacob whose name became Israel. It is to them that this book is written.

Growing up in my neighborhood and at school, many of my friends were of the Jewish faith.

Their parents were willing to answer questions from a young and inquisitive mind. I still maintain my friendship with many of them. We respected each other's beliefs. Today, I see a growing hostility towards the Jews. I would like to make a point here. G-d made a promise to Abraham concerning the other nations. It holds true today. Genesis 12.3:

> 3 And <u>I will bless them that bless thee, and him that curseth thee will I curse;</u> and in thee shall all the families of the earth be blessed.

Therefore, I have chosen to bless the G-d of Abraham and, through him, bless all of Abraham's children wherever they are!

Some of you may be familiar with a theological view held by many Christians referred to as "replacement theology." This view holds that the promises and prophecies given to Israel were subsequently transferred to Christians upon Israel's rejection of their Messiah. In seminary, I was required to study this. However, I reject it completely. You will see me prove the falsehood of that belief throughout this book. Replacement theology is a contradiction of G-d's words given to Jeremiah!

Please notice to whom these words were spoken. Are they addressed to the Church? No! They are not! Jeremiah 31.31-34:

31 Behold, the days come, saith the LORD, that I will make a new covenant <u>with the house of Israel,</u> and <u>with the house of Judah;</u>

32 not according to the covenant that I made with their fathers in the day that I took them by the hand to bring them out of the land of Egypt; forasmuch as they broke My covenant, although I was a lord over them, saith the LORD.

33 But <u>this is the covenant that I will make with the house of Israel</u> after those days, saith the LORD, I will put My law in their inward parts, and in their heart will I write it; and I will be their G-d, and they shall be My people;

34 and they shall teach no more every man his neighbour, and every man his brother, saying: 'Know the LORD'; for they shall all know Me, from the least of them unto the greatest of them, saith the LORD; for I will forgive their iniquity, and their sin will I remember no more.

Prophecy is always written in the future tense. Look at the verses above and count the number times G-d spoke of the future using the future tense. Remember, He is speaking about the future of both (1) the house of Israel and (2) the house of Judah. Therefore, if any other group of people claim these blessings, promises, or covenants, then they would be changing the Word of G-d!

In the insurance business, we looked at the past to predict a possible future outcome. All that G-d says will be done . . . will be done. Of this, there is no question and we should have no doubt. The continual fulfillments of past promises and prophecies give us the assurance that what G-d has promised that He will do will be done. As rational beings, it is important to lay out a framework for us. This may be a different perspective for you. Figuratively, it is still the same country whether we view it walking, riding in a train, or flying over it in an airplane. The same applies to Scripture. G-d's holy word will not be changed.

Most Jews have never heard this approach before. I understand their skepticism is defensive and I respect that. Some Christians who read this will be upset with me, but I am willing to accept that as well. I am compelled to present this information as a credible witness before the court of human decision. Let those who read this book decide the verdict for themselves. The benefit of my testimony is solely intended for the sons and daughters of Abraham for whom I have great respect. Furthermore, let me make this clear from the start. My intention is not to convert any Jew to Christianity. It is quite the contrary. Here is where Christians will find fault with me. If anything, the purpose of this book is to encourage Jews to hold fast to the truths to which they have been entrusted by G-d. It is my hope that all consider the information presented.

This book is going to present certain facts. All these facts are already in evidence and can be verified by reading G-d's Word. I have structured the presentation a way so as to have the reader see the ultimate destiny of Israel which is glorious! Whether the reader accepts it or rejects it, it will be their own decision. Either way, I will bless them for the sake of their fathers. May G-d protect, bless and preserve His people – the sons and daughters of Abraham!

Introduction

The information and commentary I present are based upon Scripture only. There is no consideration made for extrabiblical sources. Any decision made should be based upon hard evidence and not upon opinions or conjecture. That includes my own. Like a court case, the outcome of the case must be determined based upon the evidence and not opinions. What I present should be considered a presupposition and this must be proven. Like an attorney, I must present my case using facts in evidence while including a plausible explanation. You, the reader, will be the jurist. You are called upon to weight the evidence impartially before making your decision.

As previously mentioned, I was an independent insurance agent for thirty-five years. In my fifties, I began pursuing my Master of Biblical Studies. Most seminaries teach the theology of the particular church or denomination that either owns or supports them. However, I received my education from an independent seminary while I continued working full time. My education was guided self-study. In six years, I completed both my Master and Doctorate in Biblical Studies. I was required to learn about other religions and various systems of theology. What I value most in my education was the freedom to think independently. For example, concerning replacement theology, I was required to study it. However, I was allowed to disagree with it providing I could support my position. This will not be about Christian theology. My purpose will be to focus solely on Israel: past, present, and future.

There is a unique approach I will use to help you more easily understand Scripture. As children, we all go through stages of development. We will see that Scripture can be viewed from a similar perspective. I will explain the concept shortly. We must note something from the very beginning. Starting with the promises made to Abraham and the Law given to Moses, a clear separation is made between the Jews and the other nations. That was G-d's intention from their beginning.

The use of numbers has always played a role in G-d's plans. Consider these numbers: seven, twelve, forty, and seventy. If we look at the Tanakh, we can see it is divided into three: the Law, the Prophets, and the Writings. Dividing the Word of G-d into three parts like that does not diminish any individual part. Instead, each of the three parts complement each other. This same approach will apply to our carefully dividing the Word of G-d in order to study it better.

Let us consider the number seven. Every week Jewish families around the world gather at the table to celebrate Shabbat or Shabbos. Many would recognize the word as "Sabbath." It memorializes the finished work of the Creator. G-d commanded a day of rest for everyone. Jews are called to remember and observe this holy day each week. For this reason, Shabbat remains as important to Jews today as it has in their past. This will be important to my presupposition. The seventh day of the week celebrates the conclusion of the six days of Creation. I will present to you seven stages in G-d's plan for the restoration of Creation. Most importantly, the seventh day, the conclusion, will be the everlasting memorial of G-d's six days of restoration – the Eternal Shabbat.

Here, the giving of Shabbat to the children of Israel is recorded in Exodus 31.12-17:

> 12 **And the LORD spoke unto Moses, saying:** 13 **'Speak thou also unto the children of Israel, saying: Verily ye shall keep My sabbaths, for it is a sign between Me and you throughout your generations, that ye may know that**

I am the LORD who sanctify you.

14 Ye shall keep the sabbath therefore, for it is holy unto you; every one that profaneth it shall surely be put to death; for whosoever doeth any work therein, that soul shall be cut off from among his people. 15 Six days shall work be done; but on the seventh day is a sabbath of solemn rest, holy to the LORD; whosoever doeth any work in the sabbath day, he shall surely be put to death.

16 Wherefore the children of Israel shall keep the sabbath, to observe the sabbath throughout their generations, for a perpetual covenant. 17 It is a sign between Me and the children of Israel for ever; for in six days the LORD made heaven and earth, and on the seventh day He ceased from work and rested.'

Going forward, we will focus on the number seven. We will use this number to explain Israel's past, present, and their glorious destiny.

As the sons and daughters of Abraham continue to celebrate the seventh day, you will see the importance of this "seventh day" in Israel's glorious destiny. It is the reason G-d instructed Israel to celebrate Shabbat and keep it holy. Shabbat is not only a memorial of the Creation, but a constant reminder of the promises G-d made to Israel through their prophets and king. Those promises will be fulfilled before the Seventh Day – the Eternal Shabbat. Therefore, Shabbat should provide them with a constant reminder of their great hope. In Israel's future, they will celebrate the restoration of Creation, the establishment of the Davidic Kingdom, and the fulfillment of Israel's role as a nation of priests to the Gentiles. That, dear friend, is cause for great celebration. That is the Eternal Shabbat!

1

In The Beginning

The First Day

Let us start at the very beginning which is a very good place to start. Genesis 1.1:

1 In the beginning G-d created the heaven and the earth.

Scripture begins with an assumption or, rather, an assertion of G-d's preexistence to His Creation. We must accept that by faith. Much of the theology held by conservative Jews and evangelical Christians would be in agreement. The purpose of this book is not to provide a comprehensive restatement of all the facts. Our focus will be devoted to showing the seven days. Each day will represent a period of time or a stage; not one twenty-four-hour period.

At the beginning of Genesis, we find the record of the Creation. There is the creation of heaven and earth. Then, there is the creation of man and woman. It may surprise you that four of the seven days we will investigate are located in the book of Genesis. If you were a gardener, then you would know that it takes time to restore a garden. The weeds and the other plants have grown so close together that uprooting one will also kill the flowers. Therefore, it must be done in stages.

The book of Genesis is equally as important as its concluding counterpart – the book of Revelation. Most Jews believe the books in the New Testament were written exclusively for Christians. However, the truth is exactly the opposite. Do you remember earlier when we read Jeremiah 31? If you are unsure, then go back and read it again. Then, try to answer this question: "With whom will G-d make this new covenant?" If you answer, "with the house of Israel and with the house of Judah," then you would be right. Now, brace yourself. The words "New Testament" actually mean "New Covenant!"

Some people have asked me, "How do we know what G-d, Adam, Eve, and the Serpent said?" I like to ask them, "If there was a credible eyewitness who saw and heard everything, would you trust him?" When they answer "yes," I remind them that the eyewitness was G-d. It was G-d Who gave these detailed records to Moses who, in turn, wrote them down. So, we do know what was said and done. Why? G-d told Moses all the details face to face on top of Mount Sinai! He was instructed to write them down.

From the first day, we see the relationship between the Creator and Created. Following the creation of our progenitors, Adam and Eve, see the favorable report in Genesis 2.24-25:

> 24 **Therefore shall a man leave his father and his mother, and shall cleave unto his wife, and they shall be one flesh.** 25 **And they were both naked, the man and his wife, and were not ashamed.**

We are introduced to the deceiver who, finding Eve alone, took advantage. Adam was presumably off working in the garden. It does not take much to twist truth into a lie. Later, in the New Covenant, Yeshua HaMashiach refers to this event by calling the serpent, Satan, the "Father of Lies." We continue with Genesis 3.1-5:

> 1 **Now the serpent was more subtle than any beast of the field which the LORD G-d had made. And he said unto the woman: 'Yea, hath G-d said: Ye shall not eat of any tree of the garden?'**

2 And the woman said unto the serpent: 'Of the fruit of the trees of the garden we may eat; 3 but of the fruit of the tree which is in the midst of the garden, G-d hath said: Ye shall not eat of it, neither shall ye touch it, lest ye die.'

4 And the serpent said unto the woman: 'Ye shall not surely die; 5 for G-d doth know that in the day ye eat thereof, then your eyes shall be opened, and ye shall be as G-d, knowing good and evil.'

This is one of my favorite verses. I often ponder what was the cool of the day. I think it is early evening as the heat of the day subsides. Or it could be around sunrise. Those are matters which are unimportant as we continue to focus on the facts. Verses 3.8-11:

8 And they heard the voice of the LORD G-d walking in the garden toward the cool of the day; and the man and his wife hid themselves from the presence of the LORD G-d amongst the trees of the garden.

9 And the LORD G-d called unto the man, and said unto him: 'Where art

thou?' 10 And he said: 'I heard Thy voice in the garden, and I was afraid, because I was naked; and I hid myself.'

11 And He said: 'Who told thee that thou wast naked? Hast thou eaten of the tree, whereof I commanded thee that thou shouldest not eat?'

If you have teenagers, this sounds like the game of pass-the-blame. We can see that things have not changed. Verses 12-13:

12 And the man said: 'The woman whom Thou gavest to be with me, she gave me of the tree, and I did eat.'

13 And the LORD G-d said unto the woman: 'What is this thou hast done?' And the woman said: 'The serpent beguiled me, and I did eat.'

Did you notice at the end Adam brings the blame back to G-d because He gave the woman to him. The woman blames the serpent. Here is the pronouncement of judgment upon all three which will have its long-lasting effects. Verses 14-19:

14 And the LORD G-d said unto the serpent: 'Because thou hast done this,

cursed art thou from among all cattle, and from among all beasts of the field; upon thy belly shalt thou go, and dust shalt thou eat all the days of thy life.

15 And I will put enmity between thee and the woman, and between thy seed and her seed; they shall bruise thy head, and thou shalt bruise their heel.'

16 Unto the woman He said: 'I will greatly multiply thy pain and thy travail; in pain thou shalt bring forth children; and thy desire shall be to thy husband, and he shall rule over thee.'

17 And unto Adam He said: 'Because thou hast hearkened unto the voice of thy wife, and hast eaten of the tree, of which I commanded thee, saying: Thou shalt not eat of it; cursed is the ground for thy sake; in toil shalt thou eat of it all the days of thy life.

18 Thorns also and thistles shall it bring forth to thee; and thou shalt eat the herb of the field.

19 In the sweat of thy face shalt thou eat bread, till thou return unto the ground;

for out of it wast thou taken; for dust thou art, and unto dust shalt thou return.'

The penalty of death may seem a bit severe. However, we must see that G-d's initial warning was precise and the consequence made clear. G-d does not change His mind. Look back to Genesis 2.16-17:

16 And the LORD G-d commanded the man, saying: 'Of every tree of the garden thou mayest freely eat;

17 but of the tree of the know-ledge of good and evil, thou shalt not eat of it; <u>for in the day that thou eatest thereof thou shalt surely die.</u>'

We return to the story and find both Adam and Eve naked and ashamed of their state. Sin committed needs a covering even if it is only temporary. G-d made the first sacrifice to provide the couple with the needed covering. Verse 3.21:

21 And the LORD G-d made for Adam and for his wife garments of skins, and clothed them.

This situation now placed the Creator in a precarious position. To have the knowledge of good and evil was one thing, but to also have access to eternal life through the Tree of Life, that would make them the same as G-d. As such, He dealt with the situation. Verses 3.22-24:

> 22 And the LORD G-d said: 'Behold, the man is become as one of us, to know good and evil; and now, lest he put forth his hand, and take also of the tree of life, and eat, and live for ever.'

> 23 Therefore the LORD G-d sent him forth from the garden of Eden, to till the ground from whence he was taken.

> 24 So He drove out the man; and He placed at the east of the garden of Eden the cherubim, and the flaming sword which turned every way, to keep the way to the tree of life.

Our symbolic First Day began with Creation and ended with the expulsion of the couple from the Garden of Eden. This period of time, irrespective of its length, this is called the First Day or the Day of Innocence. Sin causes G-d to distance Himself from all men. He is pure, righteous, and holy. Henceforth, all mankind would be tainted from Adam's original sin – the desire to be like G-d. As sinful creatures, they could not stand in His presence.

There is good news providing hope. From verse 15, we learn that G-d will put enmity between the serpent's seed and the woman's seed. This theme will appear again in Revelation. Basic anatomy teaches us that the male has the seed and the female has the egg. Since G-d created male and female, He is aware of this. However, in this prophecy, this Seed belongs to the woman. At the appropriate time in the future, G-d will give His Seed to a virgin. The Seed will be hers. The word *seed* plays an important role going forward from this point. It will be mentioned repeatedly throughout the remainder of Scripture.

There is one last point I would like to make before we move on. Notice the last four words of verse 24. It mentions the *Tree of Life*. We know this singular tree was found only in the Garden of Eden. Would you be interested in knowing, at this point, that this singular tree reappears in the restored Jerusalem? Revelation is a wonderful book. The evil ones are judged and receive their proper judgment. On earth, the righteous ones are rewarded according to their deeds. Right there, in the center of the rivers flowing from the throne in New Jerusalem, we will find the *Tree of Life*. You will be amazed when you see how this is all going to tie together in the end.

During each of the seven days that we will examine, there are tests of faith. How is faith tested? It is tested based upon whether or not the person or people believe what G-d has said. Adam was told by G-d not to do something and, if he did, there would be consequences. Genesis 2.15-17:

> 15 **And the LORD G-d took the man, and put him into the garden of Eden to dress it and to keep it.**
>
> 16 **And the LORD G-d commanded the man, saying: 'Of every tree of the garden thou mayest freely eat; 17 but of the tree of the knowledge of good and evil, thou shalt not eat of it; for in the day that thou eatest thereof thou shalt surely die.'**

Perhaps Adam did not understand death, but the consequence of disobeying a direct command from the Creator was still death. Later, both he and his wife did eat. Was it disobedience or lack of faith? I suggest it was both because disobedience is actually lack of faith. Did Adam believe what G-d said? He chose not to believe what G-d said, but instead chose to believe what the serpent said. Therefore, Adam and Eve did not have faith in G-d's Word!

This transgression or lack of faith had a devastating effect for both Adam and all of his posterity. The Apostle Paul later explained this to the Gentiles in Romans 5.12:

> 12 . . . by one man [Adam] sin entered into the world, and death by sin; and so death passed upon all men, for that all have sinned . . ."

It is through the seed of the male that Adam's original sin is transmitted. This is an important fact to remember as G-d will deal with that later on. We will see in the future the way G-d will handle the curse of original sin in order to create a righteous man under the Law.

For the couple, there would be no turning back. They were prevented from returning to Eden by flaming swords which turned every way to protect the way to the tree of life. The couple was pressed to move on and so must we to the Second Day in the next chapter.

2

Conscience

The Second Day

Now refugees, the couple left Eden behind and moved on to unknown surroundings. As they walked together, they noticed the earth had changed. They would not enjoy the fellowship nor hear "the voice of the LORD G-d walking in the garden toward the cool of the day" (Gen. 3:8). Adam must now fend for himself. He was left to rule over creation by his freewill which would now be governed by his conscience. However, it would be affected by his knowledge of good and evil. We will find that, left to their own devices, mankind will generally choose to sin.

In Genesis 4, we find the couple producing two sons: Abel and Cain. The former became a shepherd and the latter a farmer. Scripture only tells us what G-d wants us to know. Its purpose is not to satisfy our curiosity but provide necessary information.. We have recorded for us the details of the first murder which occurred in the first generation. Verse 4.3-8:

3 And in process of time it came to pass, that Cain brought of the fruit of the ground an offering unto the LORD.

4 And Abel, he also brought of the firstlings of his flock and of the fat thereof. And the LORD had respect unto Abel and to his offering; 5 but unto Cain and to his offering He had not respect. And Cain was very wroth, and his countenance fell.

6 And the LORD said unto Cain: 'Why art thou wroth? and why is thy countenance fallen? 7 If thou doest well, shall it not be lifted up? and if thou doest not well, sin coucheth at the door; and unto thee is its desire, but thou mayest rule over it.'

8 And Cain spoke unto Abel his brother. And it came to pass, when they were in the field, that Cain rose up against Abel his brother, and slew him.

It does not tell us why G-d respected Abel's offering and He did not respect Cain's. G-d generally judges those who fail to meet His expressed instructions. However, anger ensued and Cain slew his brother. Capital punishment had not yet been instituted.

Time passed and we are told, "men began to multiply on the face of the earth" (v. 6.1). This was no doubt due to the number of years the inhabitants lived. Noah was five hundred years old and had three sons: Shem, Ham, and Japheth (v. 5.32). Seth, the third son of Adam, lived 912 years before he died (v. 5:8). At this point, G-d chose to limit the length of years. Genesis 6.3:

> 3 And the LORD said: 'My spirit shall not abide in man for ever, for that he also is flesh; therefore shall his days be a hundred and twenty years.'

The evil of mankind had spread because the sinful hearts of men were always seeking evil. This did not go unnoticed by the Creator. Moses recorded G-d's words for us in Genesis 6.5-7:

> 5 And the LORD saw that the wickedness of man was great in the earth, and that every imagination of the thoughts of his heart was only evil continually.

6 And it repented the LORD that He had made man on the earth, and it grieved Him at His heart.

7 And the LORD said: 'I will blot out man whom I have created from the face of the earth; both man, and beast, and creeping thing, and fowl of the air; for it repenteth Me that I have made them.'

The word "repent" means "to be filled with regret or sorrow" and "to turn away from." This was the result of G-d's abhorrence of sin.

The above verses are ominous, but it concludes with light in the darkness in verse 8:

8 But Noah found grace in the eyes of the LORD.

G-d is always patient as He works His will. Methuselah was the oldest living man recorded at 969 years. He was Noah's grandfather through his father Lamech. At his birth, the words of Lamech are recorded by Moses in Genesis 5.29:

29 And he called his name Noah, saying: 'This same shall comfort us in our work and in the toil of our hands, which cometh from the ground which

the LORD hath cursed.'

The root for the name Noah is the Hebrew word "nahem" which means "to comfort." These are the words spoken about Noah in verse 6.9:

> 9 . . . **Noah was in his generations a man righteous and wholehearted; Noah walked with G-d.**

Noah was a man who clearly stood out from the others. Many have asked the question: How many people were on earth at the time of the Flood? One analyst, Peter Goeman, in his article entitled "A Methodology for Determining the Earth's Population Before the Flood," takes into account many diverse factors. He posits a conservative estimate of the population to be about 3.9 billion. At the time of this writing, his article can be found online.[1]

The above estimate surprised me. Although the number varies between analysts, this one is particularly large. The size adds impetus to the event that follows. Here is the narrative as told to Moses. Genesis 6.11-13:

11 And the earth was corrupt before

---

[1] https://petergoeman.com/population-earth-flood (6/20/2023)

G-d, and the earth was filled with violence. 12 And G-d saw the earth, and,
behold, it was corrupt; for all flesh had
corrupted their way upon the earth.

13 And G-d said unto Noah: 'The end of
all flesh is come before Me; for the
earth is filled with violence through
them; and, behold, I will destroy them
with the earth.

The facts are clear. Mankind had once again chosen a path of evil and this evil was pervasive. G-d
is righteous and abhors sin. Therefore, He had to
respond. G-d provided Noah with instructions to
construct an Ark big enough for His purpose.

This was a test of faith. G-d spoke and how
did Noah respond? Did Noah believe what G-d
said? Genesis 6.17-18:

17 And I, behold, I do bring the flood of
waters upon the earth, to destroy all
flesh, wherein is the breath of life,
from under heaven; every thing that is
in the earth shall perish.

18 But I will establish My covenant
with thee; and thou shalt come into the
ark, thou, and thy sons, and thy wife,

and thy sons' wives with thee.

When you see the word "covenant," think of the word "agreement." When G-d makes an agreement, it is called a covenant. Covenants can be both conditional and unconditional. Consider the large number of those dwelling on the earth to be 3.9 million. Of this number, this is a tally of passengers to be saved from the Flood: Noah, his three sons, and their wives. That brings the passenger list to eight people. How did Noah do with his test of faith in G-d's word? Did he believe what G-d told him? The answer is "yes." Verse 22:

> 22 **Thus did Noah; according to all that G-d commanded him, so did he.**

For this reason, Noah is included in the "Faith Hall of Fame" that we will discuss later.

Noah continued in faith. G-d again commanded him in verses 7.4-5

> 4 **For yet [in] seven days, and I will cause it to rain upon the earth forty days and forty nights; and every living substance that I have made will I blot out from off the face of the earth.'**

> 5 **And Noah did according unto all that**

the LORD commanded him.

Noah was of a great age when this happened. Verses 6-7:

> 6 **And Noah was six hundred years old when the flood of waters was upon the earth.**

> 7 **And Noah went in, and his sons, and his wife, and his sons' wives with him, into the ark, because of the waters of the flood.**

Throughout it all, Noah did exactly as G-d commanded him. By his actions or works, he proved his "faith" or "believing" in the Word of G-d.

During the one hundred and twenty years it took Noah to build the Ark, he preached to all who would listen. Again, of the 3.9 million people estimated to be on the earth at that time, only eight were saved. We will see that faith in G-d's word and seeking after righteousness is always in the minority. Faith and righteousness are never sought by the majority. Noah told the people to "repent" because G-d's judgment was coming. They did not believe G-d and suffered the consequences.

Sin is breaking G-d's laws or commandments.

It is rejected or not believing His Words. The Mosaic Law had not yet been instituted. It is referring to the Law of Conscience – our inner knowledge of right and wrong we receive at birth. This has also been referred to as the Noahic Law or the Moral Law. Men were to live and obey G-d's moral laws written in their hearts. By abandoning this Moral Law, civilization was reduced to this level of depravity and evil. The result was judgment was pronounced and there were only eight survivors.

Picture those who had listened to this mad man's ravings about the Flood. It had never rained before. He was building a boat in the middle of the plains. Day after day he warned them. Then, the day came. Noah and his family boarded the Ark. It was the LORD Who sealed the Ark's great door. Suddenly, it started to rain. It became torrents and the ground started to flood. People who had rejected Noah were outside. They banged with their fists on the side of the wooden hull begging to be let in. As time passed, the rain continued and, after a while, there was only the sound of the wind, the rain, and the water beneath its hull.

My supposition is that the majority of the New Testament was written to the Jews. This is the New Covenant. Therefore, I will quote from Matthew 24. The disciples asked Yeshua to tell them about the end times and the fulfillment of the promised Kingdom. Here are His words. Verses 24.36-39:

> 36 **But of that day and hour knoweth no man, no, not the angels of heaven, but my Father only.** 37 <u>**But as the days of Noe [Noah] were, so shall also the coming of the Son of man be.**</u>

> 38 **For as in the days that were before the flood they were eating and drinking, marrying and giving in marriage, until the day that Noe [Noah] entered into the ark,** 39 **And knew not until the flood came, and took them all away; so shall also the coming of the Son of man be.**

Yeshua HaMashiach makes a comparison between two sudden events: one the past and one the future. Both of these are cataclysmic judgments. Each preceded by a pleading to repent and be saved. In the case of Noah, he was ignored by all but his family. All of this will be explained in greater detail later, but I want to show you the beginning connects to the end. I am pointing out which events are directly connected to the future!

Following this cataclysmic event which destroyed all living things on the earth by Flood of water, G-d made a promise. He promised He would not do this again. Genesis 9.12-17:

> 12 And G-d said: 'This is the token of the covenant which I make between Me and you and every living creature that is with you, for perpetual generations:
>
> 13 I have set My bow in the cloud, and it shall be for a token of a covenant between Me and the earth. 14 And it shall come to pass, when I bring clouds over the earth, and the bow is seen in the cloud, 15 that I will remember My covenant, which is between Me and you and every living creature of all flesh; and the waters shall no more become a flood to destroy all flesh.
>
> 16 And the bow shall be in the cloud; and I will look upon it, that I may remember the everlasting covenant between G-d and every living creature of all flesh that is upon the earth. 17 And G-d said unto Noah: 'This is the token of the covenant which I have established between Me and all flesh that is upon the earth.'

G-d will not use a flood by water to destroy the

earth again. However, this does not preclude Him from using other means to judge the earth.

The cruise is over, the passengers disembarked, and its cargo unloaded. G-d speaks to Noah and his three sons in Genesis 9.1:

> 1 **And G-d blessed Noah and his sons, and said unto them: 'Be fruitful and multiply, and <u>replenish the earth</u>.**

It was G-d's intentions to have them "replenish" or "refill" the earth. G-d wanted them to establish an agrarian society as shepherds and farmers of the land. Now, all of them were children of Adam and Eve.

The Apostle Peter, known as the Apostle to the Circumcision, wrote to Jews of the first century. 2 Peter 3.8-9:

> 8 **But, beloved, be not ignorant of this one thing, that one day is with the Lord as a thousand years, and a thousand years as one day.**

> 9 **The Lord is not slack concerning his promise, as some men count slackness; but is longsuffering to us-ward, not willing that any should perish, but that**

all should come to repentance.

Even with the passing of time, Peter assures the Jewish believers that G-d is not slack concerning His promises. He is patient and long-suffering. The Second Day was the beginning of the human conscience. This conscience is still imparted to every human born – the inherent knowledge of right and wrong. It is the same whether it is called the Conscience, the Moral Law, or the Noahic Law. Noah and his sons were instructed by G-d to "replenish" or "refill" the land.

Later, we will see the role this law will play in the judgment of the Gentiles, but for now, we will move on to the Third Day out of seven.

3

The Nations

Some readers may believe that the stories in Scripture are fables, myths, or epic sagas. Our purpose is not to provide an argument against their position. It is up to you to choose whether to believe them or not. My purpose is to show the reader the systematic structure of the inspired Word of G-d which leads to the "ultimate destiny of Israel." Much like insurance agents who explain insurance policies for a living, they are confined to the policy. I too am confined to the text of the Scripture.

The Third Day

Noah and his family, like their predecessors Adam and Eve, could not return to the way the world was before their judgment. The landscape had changed and so had the climate. The water from the firmament above and from the springs below had now receded. It had retreated to their boundaries established by G-d.

Some historians estimate the date of the Flood to be approximately 1650 years after Creation. That would be approximately 2350 BCE. Noah and his sons separated. They left to establish families of their own and replenish the earth. At this time, G-d instituted capital punishment – the death penalty. Genesis 9.6:

> 6 **Whoso sheddeth man's blood, by man shall his blood be shed; for in the image of G-d made He man.**

Again, here is G-d's instructions to Noah and his sons in verse 7:

> 7 **And you, <u>be ye fruitful, and multiply; swarm in the earth, and multiply</u> therein.**

Genesis 10 begins with "Now these are the generations of the sons of Noah: Shem, Ham, and Japheth; and unto them were sons born after the flood" (v. 1). This would be a very detailed genealogical record for a fable. However, this information is necessary. It leads us to the Third Day with the establishment of the nations and human government. As the verses that follow break down, in great detail, the lineages of Noah, each grouping ends with words similar to "in their nations." We see this in verses 5, 20, and 31. It concludes with verse 32:

32 These are the families of the sons of Noah, after their generations, <u>in their nations;</u> and of <u>these were the nations divided in the earth after the flood.</u>

Instead of spreading over the earth as directed, these nations choose to go against G-d's instructions and gathered together. Their intent is stated below. Genesis 11:1-4:

> 1 And the whole earth was of one language and of one speech.

> 2 And it came to pass, as they journeyed east, that they found a plain in the land of Shinar; and they dwelt there.

> 3 And they said one to another: 'Come, let us make brick, and burn them thoroughly.' And they had brick for stone, and slime had they for mortar.

> 4 And they said: '<u>Come, let us build us a city, and a tower, with its top in heaven, and let us make us a name; lest we be scattered abroad upon the face of the whole earth.</u>'

They came together to form one powerful group.

This would be mankind's first attempt to "unite the nations" into one.

To follow is G-d's response to this collective defiance. Verses 5-9:

> 5 And the LORD came down to see the city and the tower, which the children of men builded.

> 6 And the LORD said: 'Behold, they are one people, and they have all one language; and this is what they begin to do; and now nothing will be withholden from them, which they purpose to do.

> 7 Come, let us go down, and there confound their language, that they may not understand one another's speech.'

> 8 So the LORD scattered them abroad from thence upon the face of all the earth; and they left off to build the city.

> 9 Therefore was the name of it called Babel; because the LORD did there confound the language of all the earth; and from thence did the LORD scatter them abroad upon the face of all the

earth.

The Hebrew word *balal* means *to confound*. From that singular rebellious event, the nations were formed, each distinguished by their own language.

This was the beginning of the nations or, in Hebrew, *goyim*. The remainder of Genesis 11 follows the descendants of Noah's son Shem. There are seven generations from Shem to Terah who was the father of Abram. We will pick up the narrative at that point. Verses 11.26-32:

> 26 **And Terah lived seventy years, and begot Abram, Nahor, and Haran.** 27 **Now these are the generations of Terah. Terah begot Abram, Nahor, and Haran; and Haran begot Lot.**
>
> 28 **And Haran died in the presence of his father Terah in the land of his nativity, in Ur of the Chaldees.**
>
> 29 **And Abram and Nahor took them wives: the name of Abram's wife was Sarai; and the name of Nahor's wife, Milcah, the daughter of Haran, the father of Milcah, and the father of Iscah.**
>
> 30 **And Sarai was barren; she had no**

child. 31 And Terah took Abram his son, and Lot the son of Haran, his son's son, and Sarai his daughter-in-law, his son Abram's wife; and they went forth with them from Ur of the Chaldees, to go into the land of Canaan; and they came unto Haran, and dwelt there.

32 And the days of Terah were two hundred and five years; and Terah died in Haran.

This is certainly a lot of detail for a fable! More than two thousand years later, we will see these details repeated in a geneaology of Yeshua HaMashiach. We have now been introduced to Abram who will become Abraham. As the Third Day was the beginning of the nations, the Fourth Day will be the beginning of a great family blessed by G-d. That will be the Fourth Day of the seven days –`the Day of Promise.

4

Promises Made

It was in Ur of the Chaldees where Abram was born. Terah was the father of Abram and two brothers, Nahor and Haran. Ur was a city located on the coast of the Persian Gulf at the mouth of the Euphrates River. The remains of this city are now found well inland from the coast in modern-day Iraq. It is still located on the Euphrates. This is where Abram's brother Haran died. Lot, Haran's son, would be Abram's nephew. Following Haran's death, Terah took Abram and his family to the land of Canaan where they settled. It was there that Abram's father died.

The Fourth Day

It was there that G-d spoke to Abram. Genesis 12.1-3:

1 Now the LORD said unto Abram:

'Get thee out of thy country, and from thy kindred, and from thy father's house, unto the land that I will show thee.

2 And I will make of thee a great nation, and I will bless thee, and make thy name great; and be thou a blessing.

3 And I will bless them that bless thee, and him that curseth thee will I curse; and in thee shall all the families of the earth be blessed.'

G-d used the future tense to show His intentions if Abram chose to comply. These promises are being made to Abram personally. It is interesting to note that it is G-d who will fulfill them. Here is Abram's response. "So Abram went, as the LORD had spoken unto him . . ." (v. 4). This was just the first of the plans G-d had. Each time we will see that Abram responded by believing G-d. This theme of faith will continue. Remember this. *Faith* is believing the Word of G-d.

As they entered into the land of Canaan, G-d spoke to him. "And the LORD appeared unto Abram, and said: 'Unto thy seed will I give this land' . . ." (v. 7). This promise of the land is significant for Israel's destiny. This land will become the

34

eternal possession of Abram's seed. Many could argue that Israel already possess the land. However, the land promised to Abraham's far exceeds the boundaries of the current geopolitical state of Israel. G-d tells Abraham, ". . . 'Unto thy seed have I given this land, from the river of Egypt unto the great river, the river Euphrates . . ." (v. 15.18).

This will be an inheritance since the gift of land is promised to Abram's seed or offspring. Genesis 15.1-2:

> 1 **After these things the word of the LORD came unto Abram in a vision, saying: 'Fear not, Abram, I am thy shield, thy reward shall be exceeding great.'**
>
> 2 **And Abram said: 'O Lord G-D, what wilt Thou give me, seeing I go hence childless . . .**

Abram was concerned that a child born to his household would inherit these blessings and not his own son. G-d assured him that will not be the case. Verse 4:

> 4 **And, behold, the word of the LORD came unto him, saying: 'This man shall not be thine heir; but he that shall**

come forth out of thine own bowels shall be thine heir.'

G-d assured Abraham that his lack of prodigy would not affect the fulfillment of His promise. Verse 5:

5 **And He brought him forth abroad, and said: 'Look now toward heaven, and count the stars, if thou be able to count them'; and He said unto him: 'So shall thy seed be.'**

Notice Abram's response. This is perhaps the most important point to be made in all the Tanakh. It will be repeated numerous times throughout Scripture, but here is the first time. Verse 6:

6 **And he [Abram] believed in the LORD; and He counted it to him [Abram] for righteousness.**

Abram chose to believe G-d and G-d counted that as righteousness. That one verse should be underlined. G-d is crediting righteousness to Abram because he believed G-d – because of his faith!

Abram asked, "O Lord G-D, whereby shall I know that I shall inherit it?" (v. 8). G-d responded by dividing animals into two portions and performing a solemn ritual. G-d explained that occupying the land will occur in the future, after his death. Verses 13-15:

> **13 And He said unto Abram: 'Know of a surety that thy seed shall be a stranger in a land that is not theirs, and shall serve them; and they shall afflict them four hundred years;**

> **14 and also that nation, whom they shall serve, will I judge; and afterward shall they come out with great substance.**

> **15 But thou shalt go to thy fathers in peace; thou shalt be buried in a good old age.**

G-d told Abraham his children would be in Egypt for 400 years. They would obtain great possessions or wealth as a result. G-d knows the beginning from the end. Isaac had not yet been conceived and G-d was speaking of Abraham's children in Egypt!

G-d made a covenant with Abram. A *covenant is a binding agreement which includes G-d as a witness or a party to the agreement.* A covenant is also marked by blood as a symbol of fidelity to the covenant. The blood guaranteed that G-d Himself would fulfill the agreement. Verses 17-18:

> 17 **And it came to pass, that, when the sun went down, and there was thick darkness, behold a smoking furnace, and a flaming torch that passed between these pieces.**

> 18 **In that day the LORD made a covenant with Abram, saying: 'Unto thy seed have I given this land, from the river of Egypt unto the great river, the river Euphrates;**

Many times, we take matters into our own hands to make things happen. That is the case with Abram and his wife. Abram produced a son with his wife's handmaid Hagar because his wife could not conceive. Perhaps they thought they were helping G-d accomplish His promise. However, that was not the case. There are times when we should act and time when the challenge is too great. Then, we should wait on G-d. Moses would later say, "Fear ye not, stand still, and see the salvation of the LORD" and again "The LORD will fight for you, and ye shall hold your peace" (Exodus 14:13-14). However, to do this, one must believe what G-d said. One must have "faith in the Word of G-d."

Genesis 17 is a very important chapter as it

frames the future generations of Israel – the sons and daughters of Abraham. Verses 1-11:

> 1 And when Abram was ninety years old and nine, the LORD appeared to Abram, and said unto him: 'I am G-d Almighty; walk before Me, and be thou wholehearted. 2 And <u>I will make My covenant between Me and thee</u>, and will multiply thee exceedingly.'

> 3 And Abram fell on his face; and G-d talked with him, saying: 4 'As for Me, behold, <u>My covenant is with thee</u>, and thou shalt be the father of a multitude of nations. 5 Neither shall thy name any more be called Abram, but <u>thy name shall be Abraham; for the father of a multitude of nations have I made thee.</u>

> 6 And I will make thee exceeding fruitful, and I will make nations of thee, and kings shall come out of thee. 7 And <u>I will establish My covenant between Me and thee and thy seed after thee</u> throughout their generations for an everlasting covenant, to be a G-d unto thee and to thy seed after thee.

8 And <u>I will give unto thee, and to thy seed after thee, the land of thy sojournings, all the land of Canaan, for an everlasting possession;</u> and I will be their G-d.'

9 And G-d said unto Abraham: 'And as for thee, thou shalt keep My covenant, thou, and thy seed after thee throughout their generations. 10 This is My covenant, which ye shall keep, between Me and you and thy seed after thee: every male among you shall be circumcised.

11 And ye shall be circumcised in the flesh of your foreskin; and it shall be a token of a covenant betwixt Me and you.

There is a lot going on in these last verses. First, note this covenant has three parties: G-d, Abraham, and Abraham's seed. Most will interpret the word *seed* to be the descendants of Abraham. The word *seed* can be both singular and plural. We can take one seed of grass with a tweezer out of a bag filled with grass seed. The meaning of this word *seed* does not become clear until later. We find there is a physical mark of distinction created by G-d. It will separate those who are under the Abrahamic Covenant from those who are not. The physical mark of circumcision defines the covenant participants.

G-d Himself will fulfill the promise He made to Abraham concerning a child. Verses 15-16:

> 15 And G-d said unto Abraham: 'As for Sarai thy wife, thou shalt not call her name Sarai, but Sarah shall her name be.
>
> 16 And I will bless her, and moreover I will give thee a son of her; yea, I will bless her, and she shall be a mother of nations; kings of peoples shall be of her.'

G-d tells Abraham about his son Isaac. Verses 19-21:

> 19 And G-d said: "Nay, but Sarah thy wife shall bear thee a son; and thou shalt call his name Isaac; and I will establish My covenant with him for an everlasting covenant for his seed after him.
>
> 20 And as for Ishmael, I have heard thee; behold, I have blessed him, and will make him fruitful, and will multiply him exceedingly; twelve princes

shall he beget, and I will make him a great nation.

21 But My covenant will I establish with Isaac, whom Sarah shall bear unto thee at this set time in the next year.'

Abraham now clearly understood that Ishmael would not be the seed of the Covenant. Instead, Sarah his wife would bear him a son Isaac. It would be through this child that the blessings G-d promised to Abraham would flow.

Abraham was visited by three men who were acquainted with him. During the course of their conversation, one asked, "Where is Sarah thy wife?" (v. 18.9). The narrative continues with verses 10-16:

10 **And He said: 'I will certainly return unto thee when the season cometh round; and, lo, Sarah thy wife shall have a son.' And Sarah heard in the tent door, which was behind him.**

11 **Now Abraham and Sarah were old, and well stricken in age; it had ceased to be with Sarah after the manner of women. 12 And Sarah laughed within herself, saying: 'After I am waxed old shall I have pleasure, my lord being**

42

old also?'

13 And the LORD said unto Abraham: 'Wherefore did Sarah laugh, saying: Shall I of a surety bear a child, who am old? 14 Is any thing too hard for the LORD. At the set time I will return unto thee, when the season cometh round, and Sarah shall have a son.'

15 Then Sarah denied, saying: 'I laughed not'; for she was afraid. And He said: 'Nay; but thou didst laugh.' 16 And the men rose up from thence, and looked out toward Sodom; and Abraham went with them to bring them on the way.

The Fourth Day achieved much for G-d's plans for Israel. The day does not end because the promises continue. This is known as the Day of Promise because the LORD made covenant promises to Abraham. These promises will benefit his sons and daughters in the future.

There is another historic event recorded in Genesis. In the next chapter, we examine the significance of that event and its connection with the end times.

5

Sodom and Gomorrah

In Scripture, typology is the study of types or prefigurative symbols that represent a future event. I have presupposed that all Scripture was recorded and preserved by the Jews. Yet, Scripture itself was inspired by G-d. This includes all the books of both the Tanakh and the New Covenant starting with Genesis and ending with Revelation. We will see that two narratives in Genesis are connected with the end times.

The first has to do with the cities of Sodom and Gomorrah. It was G-d's intention to cover the earth with inhabitants. However, they congregated in cities such as Babel, Sodom, and Gomorrah. Three men who visited Abraham were sent to announce the birth of his son Isaac. After they departed from Abraham, they had another destination. Genesis 18.16-17:

16 **And the men rose up from thence,**

and looked toward Sodom: and Abraham went with them to bring them on the way. 17 And the LORD said, Shall I hide from Abraham that thing which I do;

G-d decides He should disclose His intentions to Abraham because G-d knew His plans for him. Verses 18-19:

18 seeing that Abraham shall surely become a great and mighty nation, and all the nations of the earth shall be blessed in him?

19 For I have known him, to the end that he may command his children and his household after him, that they may keep the way of the LORD, to do righteousness and justice; to [unto] the end that the LORD may bring upon Abraham that [the promises] which He hath spoken of [told] him.'

Abraham was told about Sodom and Gomorrah for two reasons. It was so the future sons and daughters of Abraham would understand they must (1) keep the way of the LORD and (2) to do righteousness and justice." G-d told Abraham, "the cry of Sodom and Gomorrah is great, and, verily, their sin

46

is exceeding grievous" (v. 20). Once Abraham was informed of their intent, the men continue on their mission.

Abraham was a man who kept the ways of the LORD acting both righteously and justly before Him. Therefore, he questioned G-d's intentions, "Wilt Thou indeed sweep away the righteous with the wicked?" (v. 23). As we read on, we should see this in the context of end times. Genesis and Revelation are connected like the beginning and end of a chiasmus. Abraham started the discussion by asking G-d how many righteous ones will it take to avert His judgment. He starts with fifty, then gradually reduces the number each time G-d agreed for the sake of that number He would not destroy these cities. The narrative is repetitive, but that is done for a reason. Repetition is one way to make people remember something important!

Abraham included the following in his argument. Verse 25:

> 25 **That be far from Thee to do after this manner, to slay the righteous with the wicked, that so the righteous should be as the wicked; that be far from Thee; shall not the judge of all the earth do justly?**

When speaking with G-d, Abraham spoke as a friend but always respectfully. G-d had patience with Abraham. Here is the conclusion of their discussion. Verses 32-33:

> 32 **And he said: 'Oh, let not the Lord be angry, and I will speak yet but this once. Peradventure [Perhaps] ten shall be found there.' And He said: 'I will not destroy it for the ten's sake.'**

> 33 **And the LORD went His way, as soon as He had left off speaking to Abraham; and Abraham returned unto his place.**

Abraham was able to convince G-d to repent. Here, the word "repent" means "to change one's mind or direction." G-d agreed, if ten righteous people were found in Sodom and Gomorrah, then He would not destroy these cities. He did this for Abraham's benefit knowing that ten righteous would not be found.

This is a wonderful story of G-d's patience, compassion and His righteous judgment. Such will be His judgment in end times. The entire book of Genesis is well worth reading. However, we must continue forward highlighting only pertinent details to achieve our ultimate purpose. That purpose is to show the fulfillment of G-d's promises and prophecies He made to Israel – the sons and daughters of Abraham.

After the destruction was over, we read in Genesis 19.27-28:

> 27 **And Abraham got up early in the morning to the place where he had stood before the LORD.**
>
> 28 **And he looked out toward Sodom and Gomorrah, and toward all the land of the Plain, and beheld, and, lo, the smoke of the land went up as the smoke of a furnace.**

Earlier, we learned about the New Covenant in which G-d said, "I will make a new covenant with the house of Israel, and with the house of Judah . . ." (Jer. 31.31). There will be nine references made to Sodom and Gomorrah in the books of the New Covenant. All of the references concern the future judgment. In the days of Noah, G-d sent a flood of water, but He promised this would not happen again. The judgment of Sodom and Gomorrah was the raining down of fire and brimstone. There is a reason that G-d did not promise this judgment would not occur again.

We considered two historical records that

many believe to be only fables. They may believe whatever they choose. Those who have faith in the Word of G-d believe they are true. Yeshua Ha-Mashiach, when pressed by the Pharisees as to when the kingdom would come, answered them at length. The Apostle Luke, a Grecian Jew, recorded Yeshua's response in Luke 17.26-30:

> 26 **And as it was in the days of Noe [Noah], so shall it be also in the days of the Son of man. 27 They did eat, they drank, they married wives, they were given in marriage, until the day that Noe entered into the ark, and the flood came, and destroyed them all.**
>
> 28 <u>**Likewise**</u> **also as it was in the days of Lot; they did eat, they drank, they bought, they sold, they planted, they builded;**
>
> 29 **But the same day that Lot went out of Sodom it rained fire and brimstone from heaven, and destroyed them all. 30 Even [that is to say] thus shall it be in the day when the Son of man is re-vealed.**

Yeshua spoke to those who were familiar with the writings of the Law, the Writings, and the Prophets.

Therefore, He was clearly not addressing Gentiles. Later in the book, we will look at these verses again, but, for now, we must continue.

Years may pass, but G-d always remembers His promises. Genesis 21:1-5

> 1 **And the LORD remembered Sarah as He had said, and the LORD did unto Sarah as He had spoken.** 2 **And Sarah conceived, and bore Abraham a son in his old age, at the set time of which G-d had spoken to him.**
>
> 3 **And Abraham called the name of his son that was born unto him, whom Sarah bore to him, Isaac.** 4 <u>**And Abraham circumcised his son Isaac when he was eight days old, as G-d had commanded him.**</u> 5 **And Abraham was a hundred years old, when his son Isaac was born unto him.**

Abraham would now have a legitimate heir according to the promise through his wife Sarah. The promise G-d made to Abraham would be fulfilled. His heir would provide offspring to carry on the promise because G-d fulfilled that promise Himself. Even at their advanced ages, Abraham and Sarah had their son.

Abraham had faith and believed what G-od said. However, G-d would test the depth of Abraham's faith. We will see how Abraham passed his greatest test of faith in the next chapter.

6

The Sacrifice Of Isaac

Scripture is filled with typologies which are prefigurative images or symbols. They are representative of future events. We will consider them in the narrative that follows. This was the ultimate test of Abraham's faith. Did he really believe the Word of G-d? Genesis 22.1-2:

> 1 And it came to pass after these things, that G-d did <u>prove</u> [test] Abraham, and said unto him: 'Abraham'; and he said: 'Here am I.'

> 2 And He said: 'Take now thy son, thine only son, whom thou lovest, even [that is to say] Isaac, and get thee into the land of Moriah; and offer him there for a burnt-offering upon one of the mountains which I will tell thee of.'

We find from the text that Abraham does not question G-d. Is this obedience evidence of his faith and trust? I believe it is. To what extent will Abraham allow his "faith" to be tested? Verses 3-6:

> 3 And Abraham rose early in the morning, and saddled his ass, and took two of his young men with him, and Isaac his son; and he cleaved the wood for the burnt-offering, and rose up, and went unto the place of which G-d had told him. 4 On the third day Abraham lifted up his eyes, and saw the place afar off.

> 5 And Abraham said unto his young men: 'Abide ye here with the ass, and I and the lad will go yonder; and we will worship, and come back to you.'

> 6 And Abraham took the wood of the burnt-offering, and laid it upon Isaac his son; and he took in his hand the fire and the knife; and they went both of them together.

Abraham acted without hesitation to accomplish what G-d had told him. Now, we listen to the dialog between father and son. Verse 7:

> 7 And Isaac spoke unto Abraham his father, and said: 'My father.' And he

said: 'Here am I, my son.' And he said: 'Behold the fire and the wood; but where is the lamb for a burnt-offering?'

Certainly, Isaac was old enough to ask this question, but notice the choice of words in Abraham's response. Verse 8:

> 8 And Abraham said: '<u>G-d will provide Himself the lamb</u> for a burnt-offering, my son.' So they went both of them together.

Abraham's mind must have been flooded with thoughts as he walked with his only son, the heir to the promises. Verse 9-10:

> 9 And they came to the place which G-d had told him of; and Abraham built the altar there, and laid the wood in order, and bound Isaac his son, and laid him on the altar, upon the wood.

> 10 And Abraham stretched forth his hand, and took the knife to slay his son.

At this point, Abraham was committed. He did not turn or waver. G-d saw Abraham would give his only son as a sacrifice if that is what G-d instructed him to do. It was G-d Who was the eyewitness, reporting the exact words spoken. Later, it would be Moses who recorded them for us. Here is G-d's response to this "demonstration of faith" by Abraham's actions. Verses 11-12:

> **11 And the angel of the LORD called unto him out of heaven, and said: 'Abraham, Abraham.' And he said: 'Here am I.'**

> **12 And he said: 'Lay not thy hand upon the lad, neither do thou any thing unto him; for now I know that thou art a G-d-fearing man, seeing thou hast not withheld thy son, thine only son, from Me.'**

G-d did provide the sacrifice – a ram. Verses 13:

> **13 And Abraham lifted up his eyes, and looked, and behold behind him a ram caught in the thicket by his horns. And Abraham went and took the ram, and offered him up for a burnt-offering in the stead of his son.**

The place where this occurred has a special meaning. It was appropriately called "The LORD provides." The word "angel" can be translated as "messenger." Look at the blessings that flow from G-d to Abraham! This "messenger" of the LORD spoke again. Verses 15-18

> **15 And the angel of the LORD called unto Abraham a second time out of heaven, 16 and said: 'By Myself have I sworn, saith the LORD, because thou hast done this thing, and hast not withheld thy son, thine only son,**
>
> **17 that in blessing I will bless thee, and in multiplying I will multiply thy seed as the stars of the heaven, and as the sand which is upon the seashore; and thy seed shall possess the gate of his enemies; 18 and in thy seed shall all the nations of the earth be blessed; because thou hast hearkened to My voice.'**

Abraham's faith was tested. He believed what G-d said. Faith is believing the Word of G-d. Verse 18 bears proof of this, "because thou hast hearkened to My voice." Abraham believed G-d that Isaac would be his heir. If G-d told Abraham to slay his son, then G-d would raise him from the dead in order for His promises to be fulfilled. That was the great test of Abraham's "faith."

Adam lacked faith. He and his wife rejected G-d's Word and chose to sin against Him. Noah listened and obeyed G-d's Word. He, his sons, and their wives were saved from the Flood. Abraham, from the beginning of his relationship with G-d, "believed in the LORD; and He counted it to him for righteousness" (Gen. 15:6). Abraham's faith was tested. He did not withhold his son – his only son – from G-d. Now, look again in verses 15-18 to see what Abraham and his children will receive. Why? It was because of Abraham's faith!

It is critical to see the correlation between faith in G-d's Word and righteousness; the correlation between faith in G-d's Word and the blessings promised to Israel!

7

Jacob Becomes Israel

The information below will be important later on when we look at the writings of the New Covenant. The words "the fathers" will be used. These words are a direct reference to *Abraham, Isaac, and Jacob*. It may indirectly include important historical figures in Israel's history such as Moses and King David.

Jacob played an important role as his children expanded this family into a great nation. Here is the story of how Jacob's name became Israel. Genesis 32.25-30:

> 25 And Jacob was left alone; and there wrestled a man with him until the breaking of the day. 26 And when he saw that he prevailed not against him, he touched the hollow of his thigh; and the hollow of Jacob's thigh was strained, as he wrestled with him.
>
> 27 And he said: 'Let me go, for the day

breaketh.' And he said: 'I will not let thee go, except thou bless me.' 28 And he said unto him: 'What is thy name?' And be said: 'Jacob.' 29 And he said: 'Thy name shall be called no more Jacob, but Israel; for thou hast striven with G-d and with men, and hast prevailed.'

30 And Jacob asked him, and said: 'Tell me, I pray thee, thy name.' And he said: 'Wherefore is it that thou dost ask after my name?' And he blessed him there.

Jacob memorialized this encounter by naming this place "Peniel" which means "the face of G-d." Verse 32.31:

31 And Jacob called the name of the place Peniel: 'for I have seen G-d face to face, and my life is preserved.'

Jacob had dispersed his family in anticipation of meeting his brother Esau and was left alone. It was during this time that Jacob had this encounter. Many will argue that it says Jacob wrestled with "a man" (v. 25). We are told this man ". . . touched the hollow of his thigh; and the hollow of Jacob's thigh was strained" (v. 26). Being held by Jacob, this "man" demanded to be released. Jacob's response was ". . . I will not let thee go, except thou bless me" (v. 27). Some argue that if this man was G-d, He would not have asked the question, "'What is thy name?" G-d is all knowing. Consider Genesis 3.8-9:

8 And they heard the voice of the LORD G-d walking in the garden toward the cool of the day; and the man and his wife hid themselves from the presence of the LORD G-d amongst the trees of the garden.

9 And the LORD G-d called unto the man, and said unto him: 'Where art thou?'

G-d knew where the fallen couple were. However, He wanted to hear them speak. It is the same here with Jacob. He wanted to hear Jacob speak his name. Upon hearing it, He then proclaimed ". . . Thy name shall be called no more Jacob, but Israel; for thou hast striven with G-d and with men, and hast prevailed" (v. 29). Did you notice that G-d did not answer Israel's question concerning His name? It would be Moses' privilege to receive the answer to that question.

In Genesis 35, G-d confirms His blessings to Jacob, now called Israel. Verses 9-12:

9 And G-d appeared unto Jacob again, when he came from Paddan-aram, and blessed him. 10 And G-d said unto him: 'Thy name is Jacob: thy name shall not be called any more Jacob, but Israel shall be thy name'; and He called his name Israel.

11 And G-d said unto him: 'I am G-d Almighty. Be fruitful and multiply; a nation and a company of nations shall be of thee, and kings shall come out of thy loins; 12 and the land which I gave unto Abraham and Isaac, to thee I will give it, and to thy seed after thee will I give the land.'

The blessings and promises given to Abraham and Isaac are reaffirmed. They will flow to Israel and his seed.

Much has happened in the Fourth Day. Genesis is an excellent book which explains much of what will follow in Scripture even to the end times. Everyone should read the entire book. However, for our purpose, we will continue to look at selected text. This approach should not diminish the value of any other. This is done to sketch out a framework for the seven days leading to Israel's destiny. The skeleton hanging in a doctor's office shows the framework of the human body. We are creating a biblical framework. As we read and study Scripture, we can understand the text by understanding the framework.

There is one more event in the Day of Promise that I would like us to examine.

8

Joseph In Egypt

We are still on the Day of Promise. The promises given to Abraham were confirmed with his son Isaac and, then again, with his son Israel. This occurred before the Mosaic Law was instituted. Years ago, my primary care physician was a devout Jew who I highly respected. In one of our conversations, I asked him if salvation comes from the Law. He thought about it and he responded, "Yes." I asked, "If Abraham was the father of Israel, then how was he saved?" He looked at me and then I quoted Genesis 15.6:

> 6 **And he [Abram] believed in the LORD; and He counted it to him [Abram] for righteousness.**

What followed was a friendly and very interesting conversation. I think that verse is overlooked by many Jews and Christians alike.

The complete story of Joseph starts in Genesis 37 when Joseph was seventeen. Although the entire story honors G-d and reveals Joseph's faithfulness, we will only look at one aspect of this story. It will be important later to understand the fulfillment of G-d's promises to Israel. Remember, Abraham initially received the promise by faith. The story of Joseph is about another man of faith. The book of Hebrews in the New Covenant includes an entire chapter dedicated to the "Faith Hall of Fame." All those mentioned are Jews whose great faith exemplified their faith by their actions.

For me to summarize the events of Joseph's life prior to where we will pick up his story would take the focus from our purpose. From Joseph's humble beginning, the story recounts how Joseph became the second in command in Pharoah's court. Later, we will see a similar scenario. The Prophet Daniel who, like Joseph, was a man of faith and highly favored by G-d.

Joseph's father Jacob was still in Canaan with his family during a great famine. Genesis 42:1-3:

1 **Now Jacob saw that there was corn in Egypt, and Jacob said unto his sons: 'Why do ye look one upon another?'**

2 **And he said: 'Behold, I have heard**

**that there is corn in Egypt. Get you
down thither, and buy for us from
thence; that we may live, and not die.'
3 And Joseph's ten brethren went down
to buy corn from Egypt.**

Jacob had twelve sons including. Joseph who was
presumed dead by his father. When he was young,
he was sold into slavery by his brothers. The family
was suffering from a severe famine. So, Jacob sent
ten of his sons to Egypt to seek food. Do you remember the prophecy G-d gave Abraham? It foretold of this. Genesis 15:13-14:

**13 And He [G-d] said unto Abram:
'Know of a surety that <u>thy seed shall be
a stranger in a land that is not theirs</u>,
and <u>shall serve them</u>; and they <u>shall afflict them</u> four hundred years;**

**14 and also that nation, whom they
shall serve, will I judge; and <u>afterward
shall they come out with great substance.</u>**

Here, G-d used the word "surety" to mean as
"a guaranty" of the promise He made to Abraham.
Those in the future can look back and know that
G-d foreknew the situation they would find themselves in. Irrespective of their circumstances, G-d's

promises remain guaranteed. The prophecy also predicted the timeframe of "four hundred years." When Israel remembers their afflictions, they can also remember G-d's surety was given to Abraham so many years ago.

Since Jacob believed that his son Joseph was dead, he would not send his youngest son Benjamin with his brothers. Genesis 42.6-8:

> 6 And Joseph was the governor over the land; he it was that sold to all the people of the land. And Joseph's brethren came, and bowed down to him with their faces to the earth.

> 7 And Joseph saw his brethren, and he knew them, but made himself strange unto them, and spoke roughly with them; and he said unto them: 'Whence come ye?' And they said: 'From the land of Canaan to buy food.' 8 And Joseph knew his brethren, but they knew him not.

His brothers had not seen Joseph for many years. Therefore, he was "strange" or "unrecognizable" to them. Remember Joseph's rank and position. He was certainly not dressed as a common shepherd.

The story continues with great intrigue. Joseph accused them of being spies. An agreement is made to let them go with the food. This is the report they gave their father when they returned to him. Verses 42:29-35:

29 And they came unto Jacob their father unto the land of Canaan, and told him all that had befallen them, saying: 30 'The man, the lord of the land, spoke roughly with us, and took us for spies of the country.

31 And we said unto him: We are upright men; we are no spies. 32 We are twelve brethren, sons of our father; one is not, and the youngest is this day with our father in the land of Canaan.

33 And the man, the lord of the land, said unto us: Hereby shall I know that ye are upright men: leave one of your brethren with me, and take corn for the famine of your houses, and go your way.

34 And bring your youngest brother unto me; then shall I know that ye are no spies, but that ye are upright men; so will I deliver you your brother, and ye

shall traffic [do business] in the land.'

35 And it came to pass as they emptied their sacks, that, behold, every man's bundle of money was in his sack; and when they and their father saw their bundles of money, they were afraid.

Joseph wielded the power of the Egyptian Pharoah who, at that time, was a most powerful ruler. They had good reason to be afraid. The famine continued. Verses 43.1-5:

1 And the famine was sore in the land. 2 And it came to pass, when they had eaten up the corn which they had brought out of Egypt, that their father said unto them: 'Go again, buy us a little food.'

3 And Judah spoke unto him, saying: 'The man did earnestly forewarn us, saying: Ye shall not see my face, except your brother be with you. 4 If thou wilt send our brother with us, we will go down and buy thee food;

5 but if thou wilt not send him, we will not go down, for the man said unto us: Ye shall not see my face, except your

brother be with you.

We find from the narrative that Jacob had two sons from his beloved wife Rachel. He believed that his son Joseph was killed years ago and now he only had Benjamin. Yet the Egyptian ruler demanded to see this other son as proof they were not lying.

When they brought the youngest son, they left behind their father alone but with their assurance they would return the boy to his father. When they arrived with Benjamin, this is Joseph's response. Genesis 45.1-4:

> 1 **Then Joseph could not refrain himself before all them that stood by him; and he cried: 'Cause every man to go out from me.' And there stood no man with him, while Joseph made himself known unto his brethren.**
>
> 2 **And he wept aloud; and the Egyptians heard, and the house of Pharaoh heard.** 3 **And Joseph said unto his brethren: 'I am Joseph; doth my father yet live?' And his brethren could not answer him; for they were affrighted at his presence.** 4 **And Joseph said unto his brethren: 'Come near to me, I pray you.' And they came near. And he said:**

'I am Joseph your brother, whom ye sold into Egypt.

Joseph then explained to his brothers that the reason he was sent away from them was to fulfill a divine purpose. It was to save his brothers and their families from this global famine. Verses 5-8:

> 5 And now be not grieved, nor angry with yourselves, that ye sold me hither; for G-d did send me before you to preserve life. 6 For these two years hath the famine been in the land; and there are yet five years [more], in which there shall be neither plowing nor harvest.
>
> 7 And G-d sent me before you to give you a remnant on the earth, and to save you alive for a great deliverance.
>
> 8 So now <u>it was not you that sent me hither, but G-d</u>; and He hath made me a father to Pharaoh, and lord of all his house, and ruler over all the land of Egypt.

Joseph directed his brothers to return and bring with them his father so that he might see him again. Verses 9-11:

9 Hasten ye, and go up to my father, and say unto him: Thus saith thy son Joseph: G-d hath made me lord of all Egypt; come down unto me, tarry not.

10 And thou shalt dwell in the land of Goshen, and thou shalt be near unto me, thou, and thy children, and thy children's children, and thy flocks, and thy herds, and all that thou hast;

11 and there will I sustain thee; for there are yet five years of famine; lest thou come to poverty, thou, and thy household, and all that thou hast.

We continue with verse 13:

13 And ye shall tell my father of all my glory in Egypt, and of all that ye have seen; and ye shall hasten and bring down my father hither.'

Let us take a moment and imagine Jacob's reaction to the news. Having worried and fretted over the potential loss of his youngest son Benjamin, he now received wonderful news that Joseph was still alive. Not only that, he was actging ruler over Egypt! May the G-d of Israel be praised for His foreknowledge and kindness to Israel!

For this joyous occasion, G-d stirred Pharoah's heart. Not only did Pharoah approve Joseph's request, but he also provided an overwhelming number of blessings to Jacob and his family. Verses 16-28:

16 And the report thereof was heard in Pharaoh's house, saying: 'Joseph's brethren are come'; and it pleased Pharaoh well, and his servants. 17 And Pharaoh said unto Joseph: 'Say unto thy brethren: This do ye: lade your beasts, and go, get you unto the land of Canaan; 18 and take your father and your households, and come unto me; and I will give you the good of the land of Egypt, and ye shall eat the fat of the land.

19 Now thou art commanded, this do ye: take you wagons out of the land of Egypt for your little ones, and for your wives, and bring your father, and come. 20 Also regard not your stuff; for the good things of all the land of Egypt are yours.' 21 And the sons of Israel did so; and Joseph gave them wagons, according to the commandment of Pharaoh, and gave them provision for the way.

22 To all of them he gave each man changes of raiment; but to Benjamin he gave three hundred shekels of silver, and five changes of raiment. 23 And to his father he sent in like manner ten asses laden with the good things of Egypt, and ten she-asses laden with corn and bread and victual for his father by the way. 24 So he sent his brethren away, and they departed; and he said unto them: 'See that ye fall not out by the way.'

25 And they went up out of Egypt, and came into the land of Canaan unto Jacob their father. 26 And they told him, saying: 'Joseph is yet alive, and he is ruler over all the land of Egypt.' And his heart fainted, for he believed them not. 27 And they told him all the words of Joseph, which he had said unto them; and when he saw the wagons which Joseph had sent to carry him, the spirit of Jacob their father revived.

28 And Israel said: 'It is enough; Joseph my son is yet alive; I will go and see him before I die.'

G-d had greatly blessed Jacob materially and

restored to him the son he had lost. So, Jacob left on his journey to see his beloved son Joseph. On his way there, G-d spoke to him. Verses 46.1-2:

> 1 **And Israel took his journey with all that he had, and came to Beer-sheba, and offered sacrifices unto the G-d of his father Isaac.**
>
> 2 **And G-d spoke unto Israel in the visions of the night, and said: 'Jacob, Jacob.' And he said: 'Here am I.'**

G-d reminded Jacob of the promise He had made to Abraham and confirmed it with him. Verses 3-7:

> 3 **And He said: 'I am G-d, the G-d of thy father; fear not to go down into Egypt; for I will there make of thee a great nation.** 4 **I will go down with thee into Egypt; and I will also surely bring thee up again; and Joseph shall put his hand upon thine eyes.'**
>
> 5 **And Jacob rose up from Beer-sheba; and the sons of Israel carried Jacob their father, and their little ones, and their wives, in the wagons which Pharaoh had sent to carry him.**

6 And they took their cattle, and their goods, which they had gotten in the land of Canaan, and came into Egypt, Jacob, and all his seed with him; **7** his sons, and his sons' sons with him, his daughters, and his sons' daughters, and all his seed brought he with him into Egypt.

We have a count of the family of Abraham, Isaac, and Jacob who came to Egypt at the time of Joseph. There were seventy. Verse 27:

27 And the sons of Joseph, who were born to him in Egypt, were two souls; all the souls of the house of Jacob, that came into Egypt, were threescore and ten.

They were allowed to settle in Goshen because it provided suitable pastures for their sheep. From seventy souls, it would grow, over the next four hundred years, to a multitude who would be part of the Exodus.

Now, we move to the death of Jacob in verses 48.1-4:

1 And it came to pass after these things, that one said to Joseph: 'Behold, thy father is sick.' And he took with him his two sons, Manasseh and Ephraim. 2 And one told Jacob, and said: 'Behold, thy son Joseph cometh unto thee.' And Israel strengthened himself, and sat upon the bed.

3 And Jacob said unto Joseph: 'G-d Almighty appeared unto me at Luz in the land of Canaan, and blessed me, 4 and said unto me: Behold, I will make thee fruitful, and multiply thee, and I will make of thee a company of peoples; and will give this land to thy seed after thee for an everlasting possession.

Later, Jacob summoned his sons. Verses 49:1-2:

1 And Jacob called unto his sons, and said: 'Gather yourselves together, that I may tell you that which shall befall you in the end of days.

2 Assemble yourselves, and hear, ye sons of Jacob; And hearken unto Israel your father.

He described the details of the tumultuous future of each of his sons. However, he spoke favorably concerning Joseph's future. Verses 22-24:

22 Joseph is a fruitful vine, A fruitful vine by a fountain; Its branches run over the wall. **23** The archers have dealt bitterly with him, And shot at him, and hated him; **24** But his bow abode firm, And the arms of his hands were made supple, By the hands of the Mighty One of Jacob, From thence, from the Shepherd, the Stone of Israel,

Notice these titles from Jacob's mouth: "the Shepherd" and "the Stone of Israel." Both are direct references to the Living G-d. Verses 25-26:

25 Even by the G-d of thy father, who shall help thee, And by the Almighty, who shall bless thee, With blessings of heaven above, Blessings of the deep that coucheth beneath, Blessings of the breasts, and of the womb.

26 The blessings of thy father Are mighty beyond the blessings of my progenitors Unto the utmost bound of the everlasting hills; They shall be on the head of Joseph, And on the crown of the head of the prince among his brethren.

At the end of Genesis 49, it concluded with verse 33:

> **33 And when Jacob made an end of charging his sons, he gathered up his feet into the bed, and expired, and was gathered unto his people.**

Upon Jacob's death there was great mourning and he received a funeral comparable to a king. Pharoah who had been blessed by Jacob mourned also and gave much towards his remembrance. Verses 50.6-13:

> **6 And Pharaoh said: 'Go up, and bury thy father, according as he made thee swear.' 7 And Joseph went up to bury his father; and with him went up all the servants of Pharaoh, the elders of his house, and all the elders of the land of Egypt, 8 and all the house of Joseph, and his brethren, and his father's house; only their little ones, and their flocks, and their herds, they left in the land of Goshen.**
>
> **9 And there went up with him both chariots and horsemen; and it was a very great company. 10 And they came to the threshing-floor of Atad, which is beyond the Jordan, and there they**

wailed with a very great and sore wailing; and he made a mourning for his father seven days.

11 And when the inhabitants of the land, the Canaanites, saw the mourning in the floor of Atad, they said: 'This is a grievous mourning to the Egyptians.' Wherefore the name of it was called Abel-mizraim, which is beyond the Jordan.

12 And his sons did unto him according as he commanded them. 13 For his sons carried him into the land of Canaan, and buried him in the cave of the field of Machpelah, which Abraham bought with the field, for a possession of a burying-place, of Ephron the Hittite, in front of Mamre.

Although Joseph had given his brethren his forgiveness, they became concerned after their father's burial. Verses 14-19:

14 And Joseph returned into Egypt, he, and his brethren, and all that went up with him to bury his father, after he had buried his father.

15 And when Joseph's brethren saw that their father was dead, they said: 'It may be that Joseph will hate us, and will fully requite us all the evil which we did unto him.' 16 And they sent a message unto Joseph, saying: 'Thy father did command before he died, saying:

17 So shall ye say unto Joseph: Forgive, I pray thee now, the transgression of thy brethren, and their sin, for that they did unto thee evil. And now, we pray thee, forgive the transgression of the servants of the G-d of thy father.' And Joseph wept when they spoke unto him.

18 And his brethren also went and fell down before his face; and they said: 'Behold, we are thy bondmen.' 19 And Joseph said unto them: 'Fear not; for am I in the place of G-d?

Joseph was crushed that his brothers had not realized his forgiveness. He had given it to them, but they had not received it in their heart. He asked the question, "Am I in the place of G-d?" Joseph told them it was by G-d's providence. Although their evil was intent, G-d used it for their salvation.

He explains this in verses 20-22:

20 And as for you, ye meant evil against me; but G-d meant it for good, to bring to pass, as it is this day, to save much people alive.

21 Now therefore fear ye not; I will sustain you, and your little ones.' And he comforted them, and spoke kindly unto them. 22 And Joseph dwelt in Egypt, he, and his father's house; and Joseph lived a hundred and ten years.

As Joseph's death drew near, he made them promise that they would bury him in the Promised Land – the land promised to the seed of Abraham. Verses 24-25:

24 And Joseph said unto his brethren: 'I die; but G-d will surely remember you, and bring you up out of this land unto the land which He swore to Abraham, to Isaac, and to Jacob.'

25 And Joseph took an oath of the children of Israel, saying: 'G-d will surely remember you, and ye shall carry up my bones from hence.'

They promised that they would take his bones from Egypt and buried them with his father's. Later, we see their promise is fulfilled in Exodus 13.19:

> 19 **And Moses took the bones of Joseph with him; for he had straitly sworn the children of Israel, saying: 'G-d will surely remember you; and ye shall carry up my bones away hence with you.'**

The book of Genesis ends with these words in verse 26:

> 26 **So Joseph died, being a hundred and ten years old. And they embalmed him, and he was put in a coffin in Egypt.**

9

Then Came Moses

In the same manner in which the Second Day (the Day of Conscience) and the Third Day (the Day of The Nations) will continue, so too will the Fourth Day (the Day of Promise). G-d's promises will stand unchanged. There is no better guaranty than to have the LORD's word on it. This will be confirmed from the text multiple times going forward. Another word for *guaranty* would be the word *surety*. You will see this word again in just a moment, but here is an important point to remember. The Abrahamic Covenant was not conditional. In other words, there were no conditions to be met in order for the promises to be fulfilled. There is a reason for that. Concerning these promises, G-d Himself will fulfill them – unconditionally.

Do you know what the very last word in the book of Genesis was? The word was "Egypt." When Joseph died, "he was put in a coffin in "Egypt."

Abraham was told by G-d that his seed would be a stranger in a land that was not theirs. Egypt had everything to do with the fulfillment of G-d's prophecy to Abraham. Look at Genesis 15.13-14:

> 13 . . . **Know of a <u>surety</u> that thy seed shall be a stranger in a land that is not theirs, and shall serve them; and they shall afflict them four hundred years;**
>
> 14 **and also that nation, whom they shall serve, will I judge; and afterward shall they come out with great substance.**

This was a "surety" or "assurance" to the children of Abraham that the promise G-d made would be fulfilled. It also declared that Israel will "come out" of this nation "with great substance." In other words, they would leave with many material blessings.

Time had passed. Joseph and all those of his generation had died. Look at the blessings they received during the time of Joseph. Exodus 1:5-7:

> 5 **And all the souls that came out of the loins of Jacob were seventy souls; and Joseph was in Egypt already.** 6 **And Joseph died, and all his brethren, and all**

that generation.

7 And the children of Israel were fruit-ful, and increased abundantly, and multiplied, and waxed exceeding mighty; and the land was filled with them.

G-d had indeed blessed the children of Israel. These blessings caused envy and fear with the new Egyptian Pharoah "who knew not Joseph." Verse 8:

8 Now there arose a new king over Egypt, who knew not Joseph.

Historically, there were different parts of Egypt. These political divisions were always warring for supremacy. This may be the reason for the change of administration following the death of the Pharoah who Joesph served faithfully.

The material blessings and privileges which the children of Israel had received were now cause for concern for this new Pharoah. Verses 9-10:

9 And he said unto his people: 'Behold, the people of the children of Israel are too many and too mighty for us;

10 come, let us deal wisely with them,

lest they multiply, and it come to pass, that, when there befalleth us any war, they also join themselves unto our enemies, and fight against us, and get them up out of the land.'

This was the cause of the problem for the children of Israel. Abraham had been told "and they shall afflict them four hundred years" (Gen. 15.13). G-d had given them a timeline. He told Abraham of the future judgment of Egypt saying, ". . . also that nation, whom they shall serve, will I judge. . ." (v. 15.14). We can be confident of this. G-d's promises and prophecies will never change. They must be fulfilled since they are His Word! The entire book of Exodus, like Genesis, is worth reading. Again, we must restrict ourselves to the major events for the purpose of establishing a framework.

Moses was born under this new Pharoah. His mother hid him to protect him from being killed since he was a Hebrew male. Moses was put in a basket which could be compared to Noah's Ark. It safely carried its passenger to the daughter of Pharoah who found him floating in the river. Pharoah's daughter unknowingly paid the mother of the child to be his wet nurse and nanny. Moses was raised by his own mother but educated within the household of Pharoah. His mother was able to instruct him in the history of Israel. Such are the wonderous ways of G-d. Moses was being prepared to serve the LORD. Those whom G-d chooses as His servants may not be perfect, but they had this in common: they all had faith. They believed the Word of G-d!

Moses, who was a member of Pharoah's house, killed an Egyptian overseer who was beating a Hebrew laborer. As a result, he escaped into the desert to avoid Pharoah's punishment. While there, he married and began tending sheep. Is it not ironic that Moses, trained in the Egyptian court, became a shepherd knowing that G-d would make him a shepherd of His people? Exodus 2.23-25:

> 23 **And it came to pass in the course of those many days that the king of Egypt died; and the children of Israel sighed by reason of the bondage, and they cried, and their cry came up unto G-d by reason of the bondage. 24 And G-d heard their groaning, and G-d remembered His covenant with Abraham, with Isaac, and with Jacob.**
>
> 25 **And G-d saw the children of Israel, and G-d took cognizance of them.**

The word "cognizance" means "to take notice of or become aware of." As a result, G-d was moved to act. He had already prepared one man for the job.

Moses, who had received his education from Pharoah's court, was now tending sheep in the wilderness. He appeared to Moses in Exodus 3.1-6:

1 **Now Moses was keeping the flock of Jethro his father-in-law, the priest of Midian; and he led the flock to the farthest end of the wilderness, and came to the mountain of G-d, unto Horeb.**

2 **And the angel of the LORD appeared unto him in a flame of fire out of the midst of a bush; and he looked, and, behold, the bush burned with fire, and the bush was not consumed.** 3 **And Moses said: 'I will turn aside now, and see this great sight, why the bush is not burnt.'**

4 **And when the LORD saw that he turned aside to see, G-d called unto him out of the midst of the bush, and said: 'Moses, Moses.' And he said: 'Here am I.'**

5 **And He said: 'Draw not nigh hither; put off thy shoes from off thy feet, for the place whereon thou standest is holy ground.'**

6 Moreover He said: '__I am the G-d of__
__thy father, the G-d of Abraham, the G-__
__d of Isaac, and the G-d of Jacob.__' And
Moses hid his face; for he was afraid to
look upon G-d.

This is the first of many times G-d would
speak directly with Moses. Verses 7-8:

7 And the LORD said: 'I have surely
seen the affliction of My people that
are in Egypt, and have heard their cry
by reason of their taskmasters; for I
know their pains;

8 and I am come down to deliver them
out of the hand of the Egyptians, and
to bring them up out of that land unto
a good land and a large, unto a land
flowing with milk and honey; . . .

G-d's intention was twofold. He desired to (1) deliver Israel out of the hand of their oppressors and
(2) bring them to the land He promised to their fathers. It certainly sounded like a short list to accomplish. However, this could only be accomplished by
Almighty G-d.

G-d explained the situation to Moses. It was
now time to fulfill the prophecy He had given to

Abraham. Verses 9-10:

> 9 And now, behold, the cry of the children of Israel is come unto Me; moreover I have seen the oppression wherewith the Egyptians oppress them. 10 Come now therefore, and I will send thee unto Pharaoh, that thou mayest bring forth My people the children of Israel out of Egypt.'

G-d had seen the plight of Israel. Moses had been prepared in advance for this task. Verses 11-13:

> 11 And Moses said unto G-d: 'Who am I, that I should go unto Pharaoh, and that I should bring forth the children of Israel out of Egypt?'

> 12 And He said: 'Certainly I will be with thee; and this shall be the token unto thee, that I have sent thee: when thou hast brought forth the people out of Egypt, ye shall serve G-d upon this mountain.'

> 13 And Moses said unto G-d: 'Behold, when I come unto the children of Israel, and shall say unto them: The G-d of your fathers hath sent me unto you;

and they shall say to me: What is His name? what shall I say unto them?'

Moses, this great man of faith, was telling G-d why something would not work. Men of faith are not perfect. Basically, he asked "What is the name of G-d so I can tell them Who sent me?" That was chutzpah! Leo Rosten in his book *The Joys of Yiddish* defined "chutzpah as "gall, brazen nerve, effrontery, incredible 'guts', presumption plus arrogance" all rolled into one word. Yet, G-d tolerated it because He knew Moses' heart. Moses asked G-d to tell him His name. Verses 14-15:

14 And G-d said unto Moses: 'I AM THAT I AM'; and He said: 'Thus shalt thou say unto the children of Israel: I AM hath sent me unto you.'

15 And G-d said moreover unto Moses: 'Thus shalt thou say unto the children of Israel: The LORD, the G-d of your fathers, the G-d of Abraham, the G-d of Isaac, and the G-d of Jacob, hath sent me unto you; this is My name for ever, and this is My memorial unto all generations.

This is the sacred name of G-d, the Creator. It is the present tense, first-person singular, of the verb "to be." There could be no better name for Him. G-d always exists in the present regardless of time and He is One.

When we considered the Abrahamic Covenant, we learned that it was unconditional. It would be G-d Who would fulfill the obligation. Now, the children of Israel found themselves in a difficult situation under a ruthless Pharoah. Look at the next verses to see how Israel will secure their release from Egypt. Verses 19-20:

> 19 And I [G-d] know that the king of Egypt will not give you leave to go, except by a mighty hand.
>
> 20 And I will put forth My hand, and smite Egypt with all My wonders which I will do in the midst thereof. And after that he will let you go.

Moses was perhaps the greatest prophet of G-d. He spoke on behalf of G-d when he addressed Pharoah and the people. G-d gives prophets the ability to do miracles, signs, and wonders as a means of providing credentials of a divine appointment. It validated that he was G-d's messenger. Exodus 4:1-5:

> 1 And Moses answered and said: 'But, behold, they will not believe me, nor

hearken unto my voice; for they will say: The lord hath not appeared unto thee.'

2 And the LORD said unto him: 'What is that in thy hand?' And he said: 'A rod.' 3 And He said: 'Cast it on the ground.' And he cast it on the ground, and it became a serpent; and Moses fled from before it.

4 And the LORD said unto Moses: 'Put forth thy hand, and take it by the tail, and he put forth his hand, and laid hold of it, and it became a rod in his hand: 5 <u>That they may believe that the LORD, the G-d of their fathers, the G-d of Abraham, the G-d of Isaac, and the G-d of Jacob</u>, hath appeared unto thee.'

Moses did this and many more miracles, signs, and wonders as proof he spoke on behalf of G-d. Many of these are recorded for us in Scripture.

10

A Holy Nation

The book of Exodus recorded the events following Joseph's death and leads up to and includes the departure of Israel from Egypt. Many have wondered at the number of people Moses brought with him out of Egypt. There is a reference in the book of Numbers. Numbers 1.44-47:

44 **These are those that were numbered, which Moses and Aaron numbered, and the princes of Israel, being twelve men; they were each one for his fathers' house.**

45 **And all those that were numbered of the children of Israel by their fathers' houses, from twenty years old and upward, all that were able to go forth to war in Israel;**

46 **even [that is to say] all those that were numbered were six hundred thousand and three thousand and five hundred and fifty. 47 But the Levites after the tribe of their fathers were not numbered among them.**

There were 603,550 men not counting the Levites. Historians have estimated the total number, including women and children to be over two and one-half million people.

As point of reference, I searched for a known city with a population of that size. As of the date of printing, Houston had 2.3 million residents. An army supply officer estimated the supplies that this number of people would require approximately twenty-two tons of food and over a million gallons of water . . . per day. This estimate does not include food and water for their animals. This need was per day and G-d provided! The desert can be brutally hot in the day and cold at night. He would follow them providing a cloud during the day for shade. At night, He provided a pillar of fire to keep them warm. G-d provided. In the middle of the desert, He was teaching Israel to be dependent upon Him. Continually, He proved His kindness and love towards Israel.

Let us consider the Crossing of the Red Sea.

The Israelites had packed up all their belonging and left Goshen before Pharoah became aware. Exodus 14.1-4:

1 **And the LORD spoke unto Moses, saying:** 2 **'Speak unto the children of Israel, that they turn back and encamp before Pi-hahiroth, between Migdol and the sea, before Baal-zephon, over against it shall ye encamp by the sea.**

3 **And Pharaoh will say of the children of Israel: They are entangled in the land, the wilderness hath shut them in.**

4 **And I will harden Pharaoh's heart, and he shall follow after them; and I will get Me honour upon Pharaoh, and upon all his host; and the Egyptians shall know that I am the LORD.' And they did so.**

G-d knows how people will react. He knew that Pharoah would become angry and pursue the Israel. Believing they were trapped in the marshes, they would be vulnerable and easily destroyed. Verses 5-8:

5 **And it was told the king of Egypt that the people were fled; and the heart of**

Pharaoh and of his servants was turned towards the people [against Israel], and they said: 'What is this we have done, that we have let Israel go from serving us?

6 And he made ready his chariots, and took his people with him. 7 And he took six hundred chosen chariots, and all the chariots of Egypt, and captains over all of them.

8 And the LORD hardened the heart of Pharaoh king of Egypt, and he pursued after the children of Israel; for the children of Israel went out with a high hand.

Again, G-d knows how people would think and react. The phrase "the LORD hardened the heart of Pharaoh" does not mean that G-d caused him to do evil. Pharoah had already decided what he would do. It was G-d Who hardened his resolve or determination to accomplish his intentions. Verse 9:

9 And the Egyptians pursued after them, all the horses and chariots of Pharaoh, and his horsemen, and his army, and overtook them encamping by the sea . . .

There are few commanders who would be brazen enough to use their entire resources all at once. However, Pharoah was prideful and filled with rage. As a great king, he had lost face before the Egyptian G-ds and his people. He had resolved to annihilate Israel to avenge his humiliation. Verse 10:

> 10 **And when Pharaoh drew nigh, the children of Israel lifted up their eyes, and, behold, the Egyptians were marching after them; and they were sore afraid; and the children of Israel cried out unto the LORD.**

The children of Israel looked back and saw this mighty army pursuing them. Of course, they were filled with terror. They complained bitterly to Moses. Verses 11-12:

> 11 **And they said unto Moses: 'Because there were no graves in Egypt, hast thou taken us away to die in the wilderness? wherefore hast thou dealt thus with us, to bring us forth out of Egypt?**

> 12 **Is not this the word that we spoke unto thee in Egypt, saying: Let us alone, that we may serve the Egypt-**

ians? For it were better for us to serve the Egyptians, than that we should die in the wilderness.'

Moses was a man of great patience. He was perfect for the task G-d had given him. He tells the people not to fear, but instead to stand still and watch. That is it. Stand there and watch. He wanted them to see what the LORD would do on their behalf. Verses 13-14:

13 And Moses said unto the people: 'Fear ye not, stand still, and see the salvation of the LORD, which He will work for you to-day; for whereas ye have seen the Egyptians to-day, ye shall see them again no more for ever.

14 The LORD will fight for you, and ye shall hold your peace.'

The LORD told Moses what to do. Verses 15-18:

15 And the LORD said unto Moses: Wherefore criest thou unto Me? speak unto the children of Israel, that they go forward. 16 And lift thou up thy rod, and stretch out thy hand over the sea, and divide it; and the children of Israel shall go into the midst of the sea on

dry ground.

17 And I, behold, I will harden the hearts of the Egyptians, and they shall go in after them; and I will get Me honour upon Pharaoh, and upon all his host, upon his chariots, and upon his horsemen.

18 And the Egyptians shall know that I am the LORD, when I have gotten Me honour upon Pharaoh, upon his chariots, and upon his horsemen.'

Pharoah had dismissed the G-d of Israel. He wanted vengeance. Verses 19-20:

19 And the angel of G-d, who went before the camp of Israel, removed and went behind them; and the pillar of cloud removed from before them, and stood behind them; 20 and it came between the camp of Egypt and the camp of Israel; and there was the cloud and the darkness here, yet gave it light by night there; and the one came not near the other all the night.

The LORD put Himself between Israel and their enemy. The people were cared for while the enemy was confused. The story of this battle would be well-known throughout the lands. People carry tales. This was a wonderful story of how the G-d of Israel miraculously saved His people and destroyed the Egyptians!

As Israel went forward, the Egyptians pursued them. Did the Egyptians know that it was the LORD Who was fighting for Israel? Verses 21-25:

> 21 **And Moses stretched out his hand over the sea; and the LORD caused the sea to go back by a strong east wind all the night, and made the sea dry land, and the waters were divided.**

> 22 **And the children of Israel went into the midst of the sea upon the dry ground; and the waters were a wall unto them on their right hand, and on their left.** 23 **And the Egyptians pursued, and went in after them into the midst of the sea, all Pharaoh's horses, his chariots, and his horsemen.**

> 24 **And it came to pass in the morning watch, that the LORD looked forth upon the host of the Egyptians through the pillar of fire and of cloud, and discomfited the host of the Egyptians.**

25 And He took off their chariot wheels, and made them to drive heavily; so that the Egyptians said: 'Let us flee from the face of Israel; for the LORD fighteth for them against the Egyptians.'

The battle was almost over. Verses 26-29:

26 And the LORD said unto Moses: 'Stretch out thy hand over the sea, that the waters may come back upon the Egyptians, upon their chariots, and upon their horsemen.'

27 And Moses stretched forth his hand over the sea, and the sea returned to its strength when the morning appeared; and the Egyptians fled against it; and the LORD overthrew the Egyptians in the midst of the sea.

28 And the waters returned, and covered the chariots, and the horsemen, even all the host of Pharaoh that went in after them into the sea; there remained not so much as one of them.

29 But the children of Israel walked upon dry land in the midst of the sea;

**and the waters were a wall unto them
on their right hand, and on their left.**

Imagine Israel standing there and being spectators. They watched as their enemy was annihilated by their G-d. They were told not to fear and see the mighty work of the LORD. He had saved them from the angel of death by the blood of the Passover Lamb. Now, He has delivered them from the bondage of Pharoah. Verse 30:

**30 Thus the LORD saved Israel that day
out of the hand of the Egyptians; and
Israel saw the Egyptians dead upon the
sea-shore.**

The children of Israel were in awe. They had just walked on dry ground between two high walls of water on either side of them. G-d had parted the waters and some two million people walked safely through the waters. We could say that Israel was baptism by immersion. Israel was below the water level and came out the other side. They followed Moses having believed the words G-d gave to Moses to speak to them. Verse 31:

**31 And Israel saw the great work which
the LORD did upon the Egyptians, and
the people feared the LORD; and they
believed in the LORD, and in His serv-**

ant Moses.

Israel put their faith in G-d's Word! Moses had told Israel not to fear. They stood and watched as G-d delivered them.

11

The Covenant Nation

Once the children of Israel were safely delivered from Pharoah's oppression, they began to move under G-d's leading. After six weeks, the multitude began to complain. Exodus 16.1-3:

> 1 . . . on the fifteenth day of the second month after their departing out of the land of Egypt. 2 And the whole congregation of the children of Israel murmured against Moses and against Aaron in the wilderness;

> 3 and the children of Israel said unto them: 'Would that we had died by the hand of the LORD in the land of Egypt, when we sat by the flesh-pots, when we did eat bread to the full; for ye have brought us forth into this wilderness, to kill this whole assembly

with hunger.'

The LORD responds by providing their daily bread called manna, but He tests them. Will they believe Him and follow His instructions? Verse 4:

> **4 Then said the LORD unto Moses: 'Behold, I will cause to rain bread from heaven for you; and the people shall go out and gather a day's portion every day, that I may prove [test] them, whether they will walk in My law, or not.**

Each day, they were to collect their daily supply of bread, there being enough for everyone. The day before the sabbath, they were to collect two days' supply. They were to gather what they would eat that day, but no more. Some of the people listened to Moses; but some did not. Exodus 16.17-20:

> **17 And the children of Israel did so, and gathered some more, some less. 18 And when they did mete it with an omer, he that gathered much had nothing over, and he that gathered little had no lack; they gathered every man according to his eating.**
>
> **19 And Moses said unto them: 'Let no**

man leave of it till the morning.' 20 Notwithstanding they hearkened not unto Moses; but some of them left of it until the morning, and it bred worms, and rotted; and Moses was wroth [angry] with them.

This would not be the only test for Israel. G-d wanted them to listen to Him. G-d wanted them to believe what He said. This would be important for their future well-being. He wanted to show them an example of what was to come. Exodus 19.1-6:

1 In the third month after the children of Israel were gone forth out of the land of Egypt, the same day came they into the wilderness of Sinai. 2 And when they were departed from Rephidim, and were come to the wilderness of Sinai, they encamped in the wilderness; and there Israel encamped before the mount.

3 And Moses went up unto G-d, and the LORD called unto him out of the mountain, saying: 'Thus shalt thou say to the house of Jacob, and tell the children of Israel:

4 Ye have seen what I did unto the

Egyptians, and how I bore you on eagles' wings, and brought you unto Myself.

5 Now therefore, if ye will hearken unto My voice indeed, and keep My covenant, then ye shall be Mine own treasure from among all peoples; for all the earth is Mine; 6 and <u>ye shall be unto Me a kingdom of priests</u>, and <u>a holy nation</u>. These are the words which thou shalt speak unto the children of Israel.'

This concept of "a kingdom of priests" is important. Later on, we will see this verse fulfilled in the end times. Then, Israel will become "a kingdom of priests" to the nations. Their unique relationship with the Creator would separate them from the other nations. It is through them that the other nations will have access to the Creator.

The Fifth Day

Moses was instructed by G-d to deliver the Law to the people. Verses 7-8:

7 And Moses came and called for the elders of the people, and set before them all these words which the LORD

commanded him.

8 **And all the people answered together, and said: 'All that the LORD hath spoken we will do.'** And Moses reported the words of the people unto the LORD.

This particular verse is so important, it is repeated again in Exodus 24.3:

3 **And Moses came and told the people all the words of the LORD, and all the ordinances . . .**

Again, please notice that the response from all the people was unanimous. Continue with verse 3:

3 . . . and **all the people answered with one voice, and said: 'All the words which the Lord hath spoken will we do.'**

To understand what is happening here, we must examine the concept of an ancient Suzerain-Vassal Covenant. A Suzerain is a great king who came to the aid of a weaker nation. They continue to need support and defense from this great king.

The great king or Suzerain rescues the weaker

king or Vassal. The relationship that follows is that of a Suzerain-Vassal. The great king agrees to provide support and protection. The vassal agrees to be bound by the stipulations in the agreement. This was the situation in which the children of Israel found themselves in Egypt when a great King came and rescued them. Now, in the Wilderness, they were totally dependent upon Him for their daily sustenance and protection. To manage such an arrangement, there must be a contractual agreement between the two parties. The dependent country would receive the benefits. However, should they violate the agreement, penalties would be imposed.

The entire book of Exodus records the beginning of this Covenant relationship between the Creator and Israel. They would be the only ones with a covenant relationship with G-d. This agreement is referred to as the Mosaic Covenant. Israel would become a nation of people with whom G-d made a covenant – a holy nation. As mentioned, this Covenant came with both promises and obligations. The remainder of the Torah devotes itself to teaching these. However, for our purpose, we will only outline them for you. Each year, the Torah is read aloud completely and studied by the household of Israel.

The conditional rewards and penalties written into this agreement are often referred to as "the blessings and the curses." In other words, there are "if and then" conditions of which we should be aware. This agreement is still in effect today! The Mosaic Covenant as an agreement made with G-d has not changed. G-d gave Israel a chance to make their own choice – to exercise their free will – whether or not to be bound by this agreement. Deuteronomy 30.15-16:

> 15 **See, I have set before thee this day life and good, and death and evil, 16 in that I command thee this day to love the LORD thy G-d, to walk in His ways, and to keep His commandments and His statutes and His ordinances; then thou shalt live and multiply, and the LORD thy G-d shall bless thee in the land whither thou goest in to possess it.**

That are G-d's promise of rewards. The punishments for disobedience are in verses 17-19:

> 17 **But if thy heart turn away, and thou wilt not hear, but shalt be drawn away, and worship other G-ds, and serve them; 18 I declare unto you this day, that ye shall surely perish; ye shall not prolong your days upon the land, whither thou passest over the Jordan to**

go in to possess it.

19 I call heaven and earth to witness against you this day, that I have set before thee life and death, the blessing and the curse; therefore choose life, that thou mayest live, thou and thy seed;

Moses urged the people to choose life which comes by hearing and obeying G-d's Word. How they are to do this is explained in verse 20:

20 to love the LORD thy G-d, to hearken to His voice, and to cleave unto Him; for that is thy life, and the length of thy days; that thou mayest dwell in the land which the LORD swore unto thy fathers, to Abraham, to Isaac, and to Jacob, to give them.

An interesting word is used here. G-d used the word "cleave" which means "to hold fast and not let go." This is the same manner in which Jacob became Israel the night he wrestled with G-d. (*cf.* Genesis 32.25-33.)

Their sojourn in the Wilderness would be G-d testing their faith in the Wilderness. He would teach Israel to believe Him, to truth His Word, and become totally dependent upon Him – to cleave unto Him.

12

The Brass Serpent

In the book of Exodus, there is another narrative worth examining since it is relative to Israel's future. As mentioned before, typology is the study of prefigurative symbols which are representative of future events. This is a short story about a test of faith. G-d would use a brass serpent on a pole to test Israel. Those who believed were saved; those who did not perished.

Israel encountered other nations in the Wilderness. This story we find in Numbers 21. 1-3:

> 1 **And the Canaanite, the king of Arad, who dwelt in the South, heard tell that Israel came by the way of Atharim; and he fought against Israel, and took some of them captive. 2 And Israel vowed a vow unto the LORD, and said: 'If Thou wilt indeed deliver this people into my**

hand, then I will utterly destroy their cities.'

3 And the LORD hearkened to [heard] the voice of Israel, and delivered up the Canaanites; and they [Israel] utterly destroyed them and their cities; and the name of the place was called Hormah.

They chose Hormah as the name because, in Hebrew, it means "utter destruction." It was while they were on route to these cities, the people became impatient and frustrated. They found fault with G-d and Moses and began complaining. Like a stern father who is teaching a crying child, he might say, "If you want to cry, then I will give you something to cry about!" Verses 4-5:

4 And they journeyed from mount Hor by the way to the Red Sea, to compass the land of Edom; and the soul of the people became impatient because of the way.

5 And the people spoke against G-d, and against Moses: 'Wherefore have ye brought us up out of Egypt to die in the wilderness? for there is no bread, and there is no water; and our soul

loatheth [hates] this light bread.'

The LORD had poisonous serpents come up-on the people. They came to Moses and told him they had sinned and wanted him to rid them of these vipers because many were dying. Verses 6-7:

6 And the LORD sent fiery serpents among the people, and they bit the people; and much people of Israel died.

7 And the people came to Moses, and said: 'We have sinned, because we have spoken against the LORD, and against thee; pray unto the LORD, that He take away the serpents from us.' And Moses prayed for the people.

Let us consider the LORD's response. The in-structions, which on the surface make no sense at all, were actually a test of Israel's faith! That is right. He was going to test the depth of Israel's faith. Here we have that word "faith" again. Do not forget this. "Faith" is "believing and trusting" the Word of the LORD. Verses 8-9:

8 And the LORD said unto Moses: 'Make thee a fiery serpent, and set it upon a pole; and it shall come to pass,

that <u>every one that is bitten, when he</u>
<u>seeth [looks upon] it, shall live</u>.'

9 **And Moses made a serpent of brass,**
and set it upon the pole; and it came to
pass, that if a serpent had bitten any
man, when he looked unto the serpent
of brass, he lived.

Just as LORD instructed, Moses had the image of a
fiery serpent fashioned out of brass. He had it fastened to the top of a pole. Then, he raised it up in
the midst of the people. They had already confessed
they had sinned against G-d. Then, Moses told them
all who were dying from the serpents' bite are to
look up at this serpent of brass. If they did, then
they would live.

This image is not an idol or a charm. It was
simply a bronze serpent that G-d used to test Israel.
Would they listen to Him and believe? When they
looked up at the bronze serpent on a pole, just as
He promised, they were healed. Later, in the New
Covenant, Yeshua HaMashiach makes a comparison between Himself and this bronze serpent in the
Wildness. (See John 3.14-17.) His reference adds
credibility to this event not being a fable. This chapter provides another example of the lesson G-d is
teaching Israel. It will be repeated many times both
in the Tanakh as well as the New Covenant. Israel

must have "faith" and hold on to it. They must "cleave" unto G-d. There is no other way than to listen, believe, and trust the Word of G-d.

Scripture is filled with examples. Think of the faith of Abraham, Isaac, and Jacob. What about the faith of Noah, Joseph and Moses? Each one of them trusted G-d's Word. This is important because Israel's greatest testing will be in the future called Jacob's "Time of Testing." This will be seven years of Tribulation. It will be pivotal for the children of Abraham to trust G-d's Word especially during these seven years!

Faith is what separates the true children of Abraham who is the father of their faith!

13

The Promised Land

Moses was alone when he went up on Mount Sinai and met with G-d face to face. He remained there with Him for forty days. While he was away, Aaron and the people made a golden calf that they worshipped. Moses returned with the tablets written by the hand of G-d. He found the children of Israel singing and dancing around this golden image of a calf. We will pick up the story there. Exodus 32.30-35:

> 30 And it came to pass on the morrow, that Moses said unto the people: 'Ye have sinned a great sin; and now I will go up unto the LORD, peradventure [perhaps] I shall make atonement for your sin.' 31 And Moses returned unto the LORD, and said: 'Oh, this people have sinned a great sin, and have made them a g-d of gold.

32 Yet now, if Thou wilt forgive their sin—; and if not, blot me, I pray Thee, out of Thy book which Thou hast written.' 33 And the LORD said unto Moses: 'Whosoever hath sinned against Me, him will I blot out of My book.

34 And now go, lead the people unto the place of which I have spoken unto thee; behold, Mine angel shall go before thee; nevertheless in the day when I visit, I will visit their sin upon them.' 35 And the LORD smote the people, because they made the calf, which Aaron made.

The promises G-d made to Abraham concerning the land was not conditional. If it was, then the people could have lost that promise. However, it was unconditional as we see from the following. Exodus 33.1-3:

1 And the LORD spoke unto Moses: 'Depart, go up hence, thou and the people that thou hast brought up out of the land of Egypt, unto the land of which I swore unto Abraham, to Isaac, and to Jacob, saying: Unto thy seed will I give it—

2 and I will send an angel before thee; and I will drive out the Canaanite, the Amorite, and the Hittite, and the Perizzite, the Hivite, and the Jebusite—

3 unto a land flowing with milk and honey; for I will not go up in the midst of thee; for thou art a stiffnecked people; lest I consume thee in the way.'

Moses followed G-d's instructions to create a tabernacle. A "tabernacle" is a "dwelling." Like a tent, it is usually a temporary dwelling. G-d could now dwell in the midst of His people.

Moses completed the work of tabernacle in Exodus 40.34-38:

34 Then the cloud covered the tent of meeting, and the glory of the LORD filled the tabernacle. 35 And Moses was not able to enter into the tent of meeting, because the cloud abode thereon, and the glory of the LORD filled the tabernacle. —

36 And whenever the cloud was taken up from over the tabernacle, the children of Israel went onward, throughout all their journeys. 37 But if the

cloud was not taken up, then they journeyed not till the day that it was taken up.

38 For the cloud of the LORD was upon the tabernacle by day, and there was fire therein by night, in the sight of all the house of Israel, throughout all their journeys.

Israel continued their journey until they camped near the land promised to Abraham's seed. Spies were sent into the land to obtain reports. Numbers 13.1-2:

1 And the LORD spoke unto Moses, saying: 2 'Send thou men, that they may spy out the land of Canaan, which I give unto the children of Israel; of every tribe of their fathers shall ye send a man, every one a prince among them.'

A representative from each of the twelve tribes of Israel was selected and Moses gave them instructions. Verses 17-20:

17 And Moses sent them to spy out the land of Canaan, and said unto them: 'Get you up here into the South, and go

up into the mountains; 18 and see the land, what it is; and the people that dwelleth therein, whether they are strong or weak, whether they are few or many;

19 and what the land is that they dwell in, whether it is good or bad; and what cities they are that they dwell in, whether in camps, or in strongholds;

20 and what the land is, whether it is fat or lean, whether there is wood therein, or not. And be ye of good courage, and bring of the fruit of the land.' . . .

The spies were gone for forty days scoping out the land as instructed. Verses 26-29:

26 And they went and came to Moses, and to Aaron, and to all the congregation of the children of Israel, unto the wilderness of Paran, to Kadesh; and brought back word unto them, and unto all the congregation, and showed them the fruit of the land.

27 And they told him, and said: 'We came unto the land whither thou sentest us, and surely it floweth with

milk and honey; and this is the fruit of it. 28 Howbeit the people that dwell in the land are fierce, and the cities are fortified, and very great; and moreover we saw the children of Anak there.

29 Amalek dwelleth in the land of the South; and the Hittite, and the Jebusite, and the Amorite, dwell in the mountains; and the Canaanite dwelleth by the sea, and along by the side of the Jordan.'

When the people heard this, they were filled with fear. Numbers 14.1-4:

1 And all the congregation lifted up their voice, and cried; and the people wept that night. 2 And all the children of Israel murmured against Moses and against Aaron; and the whole congregation said unto them: 'Would that we had died in the land of Egypt! or would we had died in this wilderness!

3 And wherefore doth the LORD bring us unto this land, to fall by the sword? Our wives and our little ones will be a prey; were it not better for us to return into Egypt?' 4 And they said one to an-

other: 'Let us make a captain, and let us return into Egypt.'

Of the twelve sent, only two spies returned with favorable reports because they had faith in G-d's promises concerning the land. We read it in Joshua and Caleb testimonies. Notice their reports were built upon having faith in the Word of G-d. They testify that, ". . . He will bring us into this land, and give it unto us . . . and the LORD is with us; fear them not." Verses 5-9:

5 **Then Moses and Aaron fell on their faces before all the assembly of the congregation of the children of Israel.** 6 **And Joshua the son of Nun and Caleb the son of Jephunneh, who were of them that spied out the land, rent their clothes.**

7 **And they spoke unto all the congregation of the children of Israel, saying: 'The land, which we passed through to spy it out, is an exceeding good land.** 8 **If the LORD delight in us, then He will bring us into this land, and give it unto us—a land which floweth with milk and honey.**

9 **Only rebel not against the LORD,**

neither fear ye the people of the land;
for they are bread for us; their defence
is removed from over them, and the
LORD is with us; fear them not.'

Joshua and Caleb had faith in the LORD for there
was nothing to fear because He was with them.

Now, look at the response from the congregation in verse 10:

10 But all the congregation bade [want-
ed to] stone them with stones, when
the glory of the LORD appeared in the
tent of meeting unto all the children of
Israel.

From their response, they were filled with fear and
angry. They wanted to stone these men of faith. Not
believing G-d, they chose to believe the unfavorable
reports concerning the land to which G-d had
brought them. They lacked faith. G-d said He
would be with them. He was dwelling with them in
the tabernacle.. He would see that they possessed
the land He had promised.

Here is G-d's response to Moses. Verse 14.11:

11 And the LORD said unto Moses:
'How long will this people despise

Me? and how long will they not believe in Me, for [in spite of] all the signs which I have wrought [done] among them?

Here is the cause that this generation was made to wander in the Wilderness. All of them, except Joshua and Caleb who believed G-d, were prevented from entering the Promised Land. For the people lacked faith in the Word of G-d. Verses 14.26-30:

26 And the LORD spoke unto Moses and unto Aaron, saying: 27 'How long shall I bear with this evil congregation, that keep murmuring against Me? I have heard the murmurings of the children of Israel, which they keep murmuring against Me.

28 Say unto them: As I live, saith the LORD, surely as ye have spoken in Mine ears, so will I do to you: 29 your carcasses shall fall in this wilderness, and all that were numbered of you, according to your whole number, from twenty years old and upward, ye that have murmured against Me;

30 surely ye shall not come into the land, concerning which I lifted up My

hand that I would make you dwell therein, save [except] <u>Caleb</u> the son of Jephunneh, and <u>Joshua</u> the son of Nun.

Consider the consequences of the people's lack of faith! They chose not to believe G-d.

The promise to enter into the Promised Land was temporarily delayed. It will be fulfilled. However, not for this present generation because they lacked faith. This is a typology. It represents a future event of the same magnitude. It will cause a delay in G-d establishing the future Davidic Kingdom. We will not go into details of this now, but remember the words "temporarily suspended." Then, you can think back to this event.

Some will choose to believe the Word of G-d. Some will say that much of Scripture is just fables. The difference is whether they choose to believe or reject G-d's Word. The end times are coming. G-d will base His final test upon faith. Those who believe the Word of G-d will be counted as true Israel. They are the true children of Abraham – the father of faith!

14

Promises To King David

After Joshua, there was a brief period of Judges who ruled over the twelve tribes like local magistrates for each tribe. Israel noticed that the surrounding nations had kings and decided they wanted a king too. They chose Saul who was a warrior for their first king, but this did not go well. 1 Samuel 16.1:

> 1 **And the LORD said unto Samuel: 'How long wilt thou mourn for Saul, seeing I have rejected him from being king over Israel? fill thy horn with oil, and go, I will send thee to Jesse the Bethlehemite; for I have provided Me a king among his sons.'**

The Prophet Samuel received instructions concerning the replacement for Saul. It answers the question, "Why was David chosen?" Verse 7:

7 But the LORD said unto Samuel: 'Look not on his countenance, or on the height of his stature; because I have rejected him; for it is not as man seeth: for man looketh on the outward appearance, but the LORD looketh on the heart.'

Jesse was the father of several sons. He made each pass before Samuel and this is how the LORD chose David. Verses 10-12:

10 And Jesse made seven of his sons to pass before Samuel. And Samuel said unto Jesse: 'The LORD hath not chosen these.'

11 And Samuel said unto Jesse: 'Are here all thy children?' And he said: 'There remaineth yet the youngest, and, behold, he keepeth the sheep.' And Samuel said unto Jesse: 'Send and fetch him; for we will not sit down till he come hither.'

12 And he sent, and brought him in. Now he was ruddy, and withal of beautiful eyes, and goodly to look upon. And the LORD said: 'Arise, anoint him; for this is he.

It is clear that it was not the people who chose David. It was G-d Who chose and anointed David as King of Israel. Under David's leadership, Jerusalem was conquered and the twelve tribes unified into the Davidic Kingdom.

The books of First and Second Samuel, and First Kings record the life of David. G-d loved David and made a promise to him concerning the future of his kingdom. This promise was well-known during the earthly ministry of Yeshua. All believing children of Israel patiently waited for the fulfillment of this promise. 2 Samuel 7.1-13:

> 1 And it came to pass, when the king dwelt in his house, and the LORD had given him rest from all his enemies round about, 2 that the king said unto Nathan the prophet: 'See now, I dwell in a house of cedar, but the ark of G-d dwelleth within curtains.'
>
> 3 And Nathan said to the king: 'Go, do all that is in thy heart; for the LORD is with thee.' 4 And it came to pass the same night, that the word of the LORD came unto Nathan, saying: 5 'Go and tell My servant David: Thus saith the LORD: Shalt thou build Me a house for Me to dwell in? 6 for I have not

dwelt in a house since the day that I brought up the children of Israel out of Egypt, even to this day, but have walked in a tent and in a tabernacle.

7 In all places wherein I have walked among all the children of Israel, spoke I a word with any of the tribes of Israel, whom I commanded to feed My people Israel, saying: Why have ye not built Me a house of cedar?

8 Now therefore thus shalt thou say unto My servant David: <u>Thus saith the LORD of hosts: I took thee from the sheepcote, from following the sheep, that thou shouldest be prince over My people, over Israel.</u>

9 And I have been with thee whithersoever thou didst go, and have cut off all thine enemies from before thee; and I will make thee a great name, like unto the name of the great ones that are in the earth.

10 And I will appoint a place for My people Israel, and will plant them, that they may dwell in their own place, and be disquieted no more; neither shall

the children of wickedness afflict them any more, as at the first, 11 even from the day that I commanded judges to be over My people Israel; and I will cause thee to rest from all thine enemies. Moreover the LORD telleth thee that the LORD will make thee a house.

12 **When thy days are fulfilled, and thou shalt sleep with thy fathers, I will set up thy seed after thee, that shall proceed out of thy body, and I will establish his kingdom.**

13 **He shall build a house for My name, and I will establish the throne of his kingdom for ever.**

G-d promised David an eternal dynasty. We know that it will be a Son because He said I will establish the throne of "His kingdom" forever. Furthermore, this Son cannot be from any tribe. He must be a Son born into the house of David – a royal descendant. He will sit upon David's throne and His Kingdom will be established forever! Verses 14-16:

14 I [G-d] will be **to him** for a father, and **he** shall be to Me for **a son**; if **he** commit iniquity, I will chasten **him**

with the rod of men, and with the stripes of the children of men; 15 but My mercy shall not depart from <u>him</u>, as I took it from Saul, whom I put away before thee.

16 And thy house and thy kingdom shall be made sure for ever before thee; thy throne shall be established for ever.'

The children of Israel continue to earnestly look for this heir. All of them are aware of this promise. Soon, we will see how important this promise is to their future.

Following Solomon's death, David's Kingdom was divided between Solomon's two sons: Rehoboam and Jeroboam. The ten northern tribes followed Rehoboam who revolted and fought against his brother. The two tribes of Benjamin and Judah remained under Rehoboam who was the rightful king with Jerusalem as its capitol. These two tribes are collectively referred to as "Judah." The northern tribes had Samaria as its capitol. They are referred to as "Israel" or the northern kingdom. All this will become important later when we see how G-d uses these two names.

The history of the northern kingdom was

short. They worshipped false G-ds and, after repeated warnings, G-d brought judgment upon them by the Assyrians. Israel was defeated in approximately 722 BCE. Their captors used assimilation into other cultures as a means for them to lose their identity. For that reason, they are sometimes referred to as "the lost tribes." The Jews who remained were considered to be half-breeds and looked down upon by the other Jews. The name "Jew" is derived from the tribe of "Judah." Using the name Judah generally includes both the tribes of Judah and Benjamin.

The Davidic Promise of an eternal heir for David's throne was always in the minds of faithful Jews. It was their hope that G-d would continue with His holy nation. That resonated especially during the Roman occupation. Their expectations were of a mighty warrior-king coming to save them from their oppressors. That will happen, but not until much later. G-d must first accomplish other objectives. First and foremost in the minds of the Jews was the coming King and David's eternal Kingdom.

The two remaining tribes of Benjamin and Judah continued to operate the temple sacrifices in Jerusalem. They also begin to worship false G-ds and idols similar to its northern cousins. G-d sent them prophets warning them of impending judgment if they did not repent. They ignored the prophets and continued to disobey G-d. This resulted in what is referred to as the "Babylonian Exile" or "Babylonian Captivity." This occurred in approximately 586 BCE. The Prophet Danial was one of many young princes carried off to Babylon by King Nebuchadnezzar's army. The book of Daniel provides important keys to understanding the end times. We will look at Daniel in the next chapter.

15

The Prophet Daniel

I teach classes on the book of Revelation which is the last book in the New Covenant. I remember one class which was a group of mostly blue-collar workers. I started by saying, "Please turn to the book of Daniel." There was utter pandemonium like I was changing the subject matter. So, I will tell you the same thing I told them. To understand Revelation or the end times, we must begin with the book of Daniel! Whether you are a Christian or a Jew, if you want to understand the end times, then Daniel is your man! However, before we start looking at key verses, allow me to provide a brief introduction to Daniel the Prophet.

It is interesting in the Hebrew Scripture the book of Daniel is found under the Writings, like Psalms and Proverbs, and not the Prophets. Like Joseph, Daniel's life was the result of circumstances beyond his control. The current king of Israel had displeased G-d and, as a result, he was defeated. The majority of Israel was either killed or carried off into exile in Babylon. As a young prince, he was included in the latter group. Daniel 1.1-4:

> 1 In the third year of the reign of Jehoiakim king of Judah came Nebuchadnezzar king of Babylon unto Jerusalem, and besieged it. 2 And the Lord gave Jehoiakim king of Judah into his hand, with part of the vessels of the house of G-d; and he carried them into the land of Shinar to the house of his G-d, and the vessels he brought into the treasure-house of his G-d.

> 3 And the king spoke unto Ashpenaz his chief officer, that he should bring in certain of the children of Israel, and of the seed royal, and of the nobles, 4 youths in whom was no blemish, but fair to look on, and skilful in all wisdom, and skilful in knowledge, and discerning in thought, and such as had ability to stand in the king's palace; and that he should teach them the learning and the tongue of the Chaldeans.

It was common at that time for the conquering

nation to assimilate at least a portion of the conquered nation into their own society. Therefore, the choicest and brightest were taken to King Nebuchadnezzar. Verses 6-7:

> 6 **Now among these were, of the children of Judah, Daniel, Hananiah, Mishael, and Azariah. 7 And the chief of the officers gave names unto them: unto Daniel he gave the name of Belteshazzar; and to Hananiah, of Shadrach; and to Mishael, of Meshach; and to Azariah, of Abed-nego.**

Nebuchadnezzar gave to these chosen from Judah the best of his food and wine, but Daniel declined. Verses 8-9:

> 8 **But Daniel purposed in his heart that he would not defile himself with the king's food, nor with the wine which he drank; therefore he requested of the chief of the officers that he might not defile himself. 9 And G-d granted Daniel mercy and compassion in the sight of the chief of the officers.**

From the beginning of this exile, Daniel remained true to the Law and separated himself from the fineries of this heathen nation.

Like Joseph who interpreted a dream for Pharoah, the second chapter of Daniel tells the story of a similar circumstance. What made this different was that the king not only asked to have the dream interpreted, but he also wanted the content of his dream disclosed to him. Eventually, Daniel was brought before the king to not only make known his dream but also its interpretation. Notice to whom Daniel gives credit. Verses 2.26-28:

> 26 The king spoke and said to Daniel, whose name was Belteshazzar: 'Art thou able to make known unto me the dream which I have seen, and the interpretation thereof?'
>
> 27 Daniel answered before the king, and said: 'The secret which the king hath asked can neither wise men, enchanters, magicians, nor astrologers, declare unto the king;
>
> 28 but there is a G-d in heaven that revealeth secrets, and He hath made known to the king Nebuchadnezzar what shall be . . .

The content of the dream was confirmed by the astonished king and Daniel assured him the interpretation was correct. The king acknowledged the G-d of Israel and, in gratitude, raised Daniel to the place of highest prominence in his kingdom. Verses 47-49:

47 The king spoke unto Daniel, and said: 'Of a truth it is, that your G-d is the G-d of G-ds, and the Lord of kings, and a revealer of secrets, seeing thou hast been able to reveal this secret.'

48 Then the king made Daniel great, and gave him many great gifts, and made him to rule over the whole province of Babylon, and to be chief prefect over all the wise men of Babylon.

49 And Daniel requested of the king, and he appointed Shadrach, Meshach, and Abed-nego, over the affairs of the province of Babylon; but Daniel was in the gate of the king.

The book of Daniel is one of my favorite books in Scripture because he was a man of faith. This is a book that should be read completely. From his elevated position of authority in the kingdom, Daniel served G-d and His people. For our purpose, we will focus on Daniel 9. This event occurred later in Daniel's life. He loved the children of Israel and Jerusalem – the City of G-d. Nebuchadnezzar was succeeded by Darius who Daniel served honorably.

The children of Israel were removed from their land, but G-d preserved and protected them in this foreign land. We can be angry with someone and still love them. Daniel 9.1-6:

1 In the first year of Darius the son of Ahasuerus, of the seed of the Medes, who was made king over the realm of the Chaldeans;

2 in the first year of his reign I Daniel meditated in the books, over the number of the years, whereof the word of the LORD came to Jeremiah the prophet, that He would accomplish for the desolations of Jerusalem seventy years.

3 And I set my face unto the Lord G-d, to seek by prayer and supplications, with fasting, and sackcloth, and ashes.

4 And I prayed unto the LORD my G-d, and made confession, and said: 'O Lord, the great and awful G-d, who keepest covenant and mercy with them that love Thee and keep Thy commandments,

**5 we have sinned, and have dealt iniq-
uitously, and have done wickedly, and
have rebelled, and have turned aside
from Thy commandments and from
Thine ordinances; 6 neither have we
hearkened unto Thy servants the
prophets, that spoke in Thy name to
our kings, our princes, and our fathers,
and to all the people of the land.**

Israel had been broken the Mosaic Covenant.
The LORD determined the punishment for Israel to
be seventy years in exile. He had made clear in the
covenant there would be consequences for failure to
keep the Law. It was during this period of exile that
Daniel received news of the state of Jerusalem from
travelers who had seen it. This brought great dis-
tress upon Daniel. He admitted the people had dis-
obeyed G-d and broken the Covenant. In his prayer,
he included both the two tribes of Judah and the
other ten tribes.

He recounts their obligations under the Covenant, their disobedience, and then he justified the
actions G-d took to punish them. Verses 7-15:

**7 Unto Thee, O Lord, belongeth right-
eousness, but unto us confusion of
face, as at this day; to the men of Judah,
and to the inhabitants of Jerusalem,**

and unto all Israel, that are near, and that are far off, through all the countries whither Thou hast driven them, because they dealt treacherously with Thee.

8 O LORD, to us belongeth confusion of face, to our kings, to our princes, and to our fathers, because we have sinned against Thee. 9 To the Lord our G-d belong compassions and forgivenesses; for we have rebelled against Him; 10 neither have we hearkened to the voice of the LORD our G-d, to walk in His laws, which He set before us by His servants the prophets.

11 Yea, all Israel have transgressed Thy law, and have turned aside, so as not to hearken to Thy voice; and so there hath been poured out upon us the curse and the oath that is written in the Law of Moses the servant of G-d; for we have sinned against Him. 12 And He hath confirmed His word, which He spoke against us, and against our judges that judged us, by bringing upon us a great evil; so that under the whole heaven hath not been done as hath been done upon Jerusalem.

13 As it is written in the Law of Moses, all this evil is come upon us; yet have we not entreated the favour of the LORD our G-d, that we might turn from our iniquities, and have discernment in Thy truth. 14 And so the LORD hath watched over the evil, and brought it upon us; for the LORD our G-d is righteous in all His works which He hath done, and we have not hearkened to His voice.

15 And now, O Lord our G-d, that hast brought Thy people forth out of the land of Egypt with a mighty hand, and hast gotten Thee renown, as at this day; we have sinned, we have done wickedly.

Daniel continued his prayer by pointing out Jerusalem was known by all the nations as the City of G-d Whose fame for miraculously saving Israel from Egypt was known throughout the lands. Verses 16-19:

16 O Lord, according to all Thy righteousness, let Thine anger and Thy fury, I pray Thee, be turned away from Thy city Jerusalem, Thy holy mountain; because for our sins, and for the

iniquities of our fathers, Jerusalem and Thy people are become a reproach to all that are about us.

17 Now therefore, O our G-d, hearken unto the prayer of Thy servant, and to his supplications, and cause Thy face to shine upon Thy sanctuary that is desolate, for the Lord's sake.

18 O my G-d, incline Thine ear, and hear; open Thine eyes, and behold our desolations, and the city upon which Thy name is called; for we do not present our supplications before Thee because of our righteousness, but because of Thy great compassions.

19 O Lord, hear, O Lord, forgive, O Lord, attend and do, defer not; for Thine own sake, O my G-d, because Thy name is called upon Thy city and Thy people.'

In response, G-d sent the angel Gabriel. He informed Daniel that G-d had heard his request. Verses 20-22:

20 And while I was speaking, and praying, and confessing my sin and the sin

of my people Israel, and presenting my supplication before the LORD my G-d for the holy mountain of my G-d;

21 yea, while I was speaking in prayer, the man Gabriel, whom I had seen in the vision at the beginning, being caused to fly swiftly, approached close to me about the time of the evening offering.

22 And he made me to understand, and talked with me, and said: 'O Daniel, I am now come forth to make thee skilful of understanding.

The word "skilful" means "having the skill or ability to understand." Gabriel was a messenger sent from G-d to deliver this message to Daniel.

The following verses are very important as they establish a timeline we can use. He answered Daniel's question about the restoration of Jerusalem, but His answer went far beyond the question. This information leads us to understand not only when Jerusalem will be restored, but when David's eternal kingdom will be established. Furthermore, it confirms that the eternal King will be the Son of David. This information is critical to understanding the end times and the glorious destiny of Israel!

Gabriel begins the announcement with the words *seventy weeks*. This is an indication of time. Israel's exile to Babylon was to last seventy years, but the exile will be seven times longer. In the following verses, we see the number seventy mentioned again. Here, we out that the seventy weeks actually refers to seventy weeks-of-years. Using simple multiplication, seventy weeks of seven years each would total 490 years.

I know this is confusing at first, but . I promise you it will make sense. Verses 23-24:

> 23 **At the beginning of thy supplications [requests} a word [an answer] went forth, and I am come to declare it; for thou art greatly beloved; therefore look into the word, and understand the vision.**

> 24 **Seventy weeks are decreed upon thy people and upon thy holy city, to finish the transgression, and to make an end of sin, and to forgive iniquity, and to bring in everlasting righteousness, and to seal vision and prophet, and to anoint the most holy place.**

Let us summarize what G-d said will be completed by the end of the 490 years. He promised to:

(1) to finish the transgression, and to make an end of sin,

(2) to forgive iniquity, and to bring in everlasting righteousness,

(3) to seal up vision and prophet, and

(4) to anoint the most holy place.

First, G-d will make an end of sin. This means that sin would be eradicated which requires the cost of sin to be paid in full. Second, He speaks of forgiveness and establishing everlasting righteousness. Third, when He speaks about sealing up, this would be closing a book or scroll and sealing it. Both visions and prophecies will be fulfilled by the end of this time. Finally, G-d will anoint the holy place which, we will see, is G-d's Holy City – Jerusalem. All this came in the answer to Daniel's question concerning Jerusalem's restoration.

This is certainly a lot to take. It is important that you see what G-d is promising *will* happen. In other words, this is a prophecy – a promise from G-d concerning future events. You may need to read this more than once. Gabriel told Daniel to "look into the word." In other words, the angel told Daniel that Scripture will bear this out to be true. Scripture is the Word of G-d and will prove itself to be trustworthy. There is no other way to validate what Daniel was told than by Scripture.

What Gabriel told Daniel we are doing right now –looking into the Word. When we do this, we see that the angel's message was about the establishment of the eternal Kingdom promised to King David. Daniel now has the timeline in when this will be fulfilled. G-d *will* establish the Kingdom. He *will* anoint Israel's eternal King – the Anointed One. This King *will* rule from David's throne in Jerusalem – the City of G-d.

The response Daniel received concerned Jerusalem and its future restoration. Verses 25-26:

25 **Know therefore and discern, that from the going forth of the word to restore and to build Jerusalem unto [until the] one anointed, a prince, shall be seven weeks; and for threescore and two weeks, it shall be built again, with broad place and moat, but in troublous times.**

26 **And after the threescore and two weeks shall an anointed one be cut off, and be no more; and the people of a prince that shall come shall destroy the city and the sanctuary; but his end shall be with a flood; and unto the end of the war desolations are determined.**

We learn when Jerusalem will be restored as well as a reference to *one who is anointed*. We have seen the word *anointed* used in connection with King David where we previously read, "... And the LORD said: 'Arise, anoint him; for this is he'" (1 Sam. 16.12).

Seven weeks were mentioned in verse 25 and another sixty-two weeks are mentioned in verse 26. If we add them together, then we have sixty-nine weeks out of seventy. There is only one week until the seventy weeks are completed. At sixty-nine weeks, we are told that (1) the anointed one will be cut off and (2) the people of the prince ... shall destroy the city and the sanctuary. The words *shall destroy the city and the sanctuary* refer specifically to Jerusalem and its temple.

This has happened before during the **Maccabean Period,** but this does not preclude it from happening again. This prophecy could refer to the destruction of the temple and the city in 70 C.E. by the Roman General Titus. Although it is very similar to the event described above, it does not fit the timeline and the four promises listed above were not fulfilled. Therefore, there must be another destruction. Yeshua HaMashiach spoke of this coming destruction and the fulfillment of the promises given to Danial. We will look at His words later.

Who is this "prince" whose people shall come to destroy the city and the sanctuary? Gabriel used the pronoun "he" in the verse that followed. He will be powerful enough to make a covenant with many. Notice the length of time associated with this covenant. It says one week. However, in the framework of this prophecy, this one week represents the remaining seven years. Verse 27:

> 27 **And he shall make a firm covenant with many for one week; . . .**

So, there is one week remaining and we find that this "prince" will make a covenant for seven years. This will conclude Daniel's seventy weeks. Something is going to happen in the midst of this seven-year covenant. Verse 27:

> 27 **. . . and for half of the week he shall cause the sacrifice and the offering to cease; and upon the wing of detestable things shall be that which causeth appalment; and that until the extermination wholly determined be poured out upon that which causeth appalment.'**

Half of the seven years is three and one-half years. It is also forty-two months or 1260 days. We will see these references used interchangeably. Regardless, they all represent the midpoint of the seven years.

At this point, the "prince" who created the covenant will break the covenant. He will stop the sacrifices and offerings. The word "appalment" means "abomination." It has to do with desecration of the temple and his proclamation that he is g-d. This will continue unabated for the remaining three and one-half years "until the extermination wholly determined be poured out upon" those who "caused the abomination." This judgment is pronounced on this "prince" and "his people." This defiance against the LORD and hatred towards His people will result in their extermination.

We come to the end of the prophecy and are left somewhat bewildered. If this was a movie this would be known as a cliff-hanger. About halfway through the movie there is an intermission. Remember, I started this chapter with a story about it being the key to understanding the book of Revelation. That is the last book in the New Covenant.

All of the above will make sense going forward. I promise. So far, we only have a timeline. As we move forward, we will gather evidence in support of Daniel's prophecy. G-d gave Abraham a prophecy that foretold of the children of Israel's sojourn in Egypt, the oppression of their masters, and their deliverance. That was a "type." It was a representation of what G-d will do for Israel in the future.

16

Seventy Times Seven

The last chapter was a tough one because of its length and intensity. Therefore, we will continue with G-d's timeline in this chapter. There are questions that need to be answered.

Let us start by at what G-d said He will accomplish by the end of the 490 years:

(1) finish the transgression which is the punishment for sin and make an end of sin itself,
(2) forgive iniquity and bring in everlasting righteousness,
(3) fulfill the visions and prophecies given;
(4) anoint the most holy place which is the future temple inside the holy city Jerusalem now fully restored.

The numbering is mine and provided for reference only. We can go back to Daniel 9.24 and read the verses again.

Since the 490 years represent the complete timeline, we need to know where the timeline begins. G-d made King Artaxerxes the successor to King Nebuchadnezzar. This new king was favorable towards the Jews. He issued a decree in the seventh year of his reign (*cf.* Ezra 7.8). Actually, he made three decrees over a period of time. The important decree was the one used by Nehemiah to rebuild the city walls of Jerusalem. Since a city is not a city without its walls, that date is the most appropriate for us to use. This particular decree can be accurately dated to 453 BCE.

In Daniel 9.25, we are told that "from" the going forth of the word to restore Jerusalem "to" the cutting off of the Anointed One, there will be sixty-nine weeks. Now, we need to convert these weeks into years. Sixty-nine week-of-years is 483 years. At that point, we are told that something happens. What is the event that marks the 483rd year? The Jews are awaiting HaMashiach Who would usher in the kingdom. Based upon evidence to be provided shorty, the Anointed One is HaMashiach. Daniel is told the Anointed One will be "cut off" and "shall be no more." Most Jews, except the Sadducees, believe in the resurrection from the dead. So, the words "he shall be no more" do not imply that this individual will not eventually see the resurrection.

Let us try to date this. If we subtract 453 from 483 we arrive at minus 30. This is due to the change from BCE to CE. Therefore, HaMashiach would be "cut off" in 30 CE. Many believe that Yeshua Ha-Mashiach was born in 1 CE and crucified in 33 CE. That is not correct. If we use the Hebrew calendar, Yeshua HaMashiach was born in 3 BCE, started His ministry at the age of thirty, and ministered for three years, and was crucified in 30 CE. Is there any proof of this? If He was HaMashiach, and I believe He was, then this would explain why Jerusalem, the city of G-d, and its temple were completely de-stroyed by the Romans in 70 CE. That was exactly forty years after His death. The number forty is usually associated with a period of testing. If this is this case, then the rulers of Israel failed the test.

Daniel's timeline provides a framework. We will be looking for confirmations of these facts. Now, let us go to the last chapter in the book of Daniel. Verses 12.1-4:

> 1 **And at that time shall Michael stand up, the great prince who standeth for the children of thy people; <u>and there shall be a time of trouble, such as nev-er was since there was a nation</u> even to**

that same time; and at that time <u>thy</u> <u>people shall be delivered, every one</u> <u>that shall be found written in the book.</u>

2 And many of them that sleep in the dust of the earth shall awake, some to everlasting life, and some to reproaches and everlasting abhorrence.

3 And they that are wise shall shine as the brightness of the firmament; and they that turn the many to righteousness as the stars for ever and ever.

4 But thou, O Daniel, shut up the words, and seal the book, even to the time of the end; many shall run to and fro, and knowledge shall be increased.'

Michael is the Archangel who defends Israel. The period of time that he called "a time of trouble" is the Tribulation. This seventieth week or last seven years of the 490-year timeline, will be like nothing Israel has ever experienced before. As with their escape from Egypt, those who had faith were delivered to the Promised land. Similarly, in their future, salvation for Israel will be limited to those whose names are found written in the book.

I contend that the majority of the books contained in the New Covenant were written specifically to the Jews. The evidence to prove this will become clear shortly. The first four books, called "the gospels," continue the Tanakh. They refer many times to the names of faithful Israel being written in and blotted out of this book. That will be the determining factor between their salvation or eternal judgment. In verse 2 above, the angel speaks about the resurrection from the dead. He said, "some to everlasting life, some to reproaches, and some to everlasting abhorrence."

Michael instructs Daniel to shut up the words of prophecy and to seal the book until the end times. Many will run around increasing their "human knowledge" which is sometimes called "science." However, those who seek after G-d and the knowledge of Him by studying His Word, we are told, "they that are wise shall shine as the brightness of the firmament" (v. 12.3).

There were two other beings who appeared with Michael. One asks the other a question. The answer received is very interesting. Verses 5-6:

5 Then I Daniel looked, and, behold, there stood other two, the one on the bank of the river on this side, and the other on the bank of the river on that side.

6 And one said to the man clothed in linen, who was above the waters of the river: 'How long shall it be to the end of the wonders?'

The man who was floating above the waters answered and gave a length of time for Daniel's benefit. Verse 7:

7 And I heard the man clothed in linen, who was above the waters of the river, when he lifted up his right hand and his left hand unto heaven, and swore by Him that liveth for ever that it shall be for <u>a time, times, and a half</u>; and when they have made an end of breaking in pieces the power of the holy people, all these things shall be finished.

He spoke about the enemies of Israel who are the holy people of G-d. These *people of the prince* are those who will flood into the city to destroy it and the temple. Picture sports fans flooding onto the field after an international soccer game. It literally looks as if they are pouring in. Such will be the case beginning at the midpoint of the seven years.

Daniel was puzzled and asked a question in verse 8:

8 And I heard, but I understood not; then said I: 'O my Lord, what shall be the latter end of these things?'

The answer he received will be invaluable to understanding the end times. Verses 9-11:

9 And he said: 'Go thy way, Daniel; for the words are shut up and sealed till the time of the end.

10 Many shall purify themselves, and make themselves white, and be refined; but the wicked shall do wickedly; and none of the wicked shall understand; but they that are wise shall understand.

11 And from the time that the continual burnt-offering shall be taken away, and the detestable thing that causes appalment set up, there shall be a thousand two hundred and ninety days.

Halfway into the seven years, the offerings will be stopped and the appalment or abomination will start and continue until the end. (*cf.* Daniel 9.27.) The end times are approaching. Now is the time for the wise to understand and shine! Soon, I will show you the words of Yeshua HaMashiach Who states what exactly the signs of the end times will be. So, hang in here and do not give up.

The faithful Jews patiently wait for the promises G-d made to Abraham, Isaac, Jacob, and David to be fulfilled. I am telling you that you will see it for yourself, if you stay with me. Look at the last words in the book of Daniel written below. These were the words given to Daniel instructing him to seal them up. Verses 12-13:

> 12 **Happy is he that waiteth, and cometh to the thousand three hundred and five and thirty days. 13 But go thou thy way till the end be; and thou shalt rest, and shalt stand up to thy lot, at the end of the days.'**

Now, because of Who Yeshua HaMashiach is and what He has done for Israel, these prophecies have been unsealed! Right now, the prophecies are yours for the reading! Of this one thing we can be certain. The fulfillment of the promises will occur at the end of the seven years. "Happy is he that waiteth" because he waits in hope having faith in the Word of G-d!

17

The Great Statue

We began with Daniel 9 because it was specifically written about Israel's future: the fulfillment of the promises and the Davidic Kingdom. We are going to return to Daniel 2 for two reasons. First, it has to do with the present age. Second, the great statue is prophetic. It deals with the future of the Gentiles in a time referred to as "The Age of the Gentiles." We know that when we look at history, whether it be for the Jews or non-Jews, it runs concurrently. However, the future destiny of the Gentiles is quite different from the future destiny of Israel. Daniel 2.1-13:

> 1 **And in the second year of the reign of Nebuchadnezzar, Nebuchadnezzar dreamed dreams; and his spirit was troubled, and his sleep broke from him. 2 Then the king commanded to call the magicians, and the enchanters, and the sorcerers, and the Chaldeans,**

to tell the king his dreams. So, they came and stood before the king. 3 And the king said unto them: 'I have dreamed a dream, and my spirit is troubled to know the dream.'

4 Then spoke the Chaldeans to the king in Aramaic: 'O king, live for ever! tell thy servants the dream, and we will declare the interpretation.' 5 The king answered and said to the Chaldeans: 'The thing is certain with me; if ye make not known unto me the dream and the interpretation thereof, ye shall be cut in pieces, and your houses shall be made a dunghill.

6 But if ye declare the dream and the interpretation thereof, ye shall receive of me gifts and rewards and great honour; only declare unto me the dream and the interpretation thereof.'

7 They answered the second time and said: 'Let the king tell his servants the dream, and we will declare the interpretation.' 8 The king answered and said: 'I know of a truth that ye would gain time, inasmuch as ye see the thing is certain with me,

9 that, if ye make not known unto me the dream, there is but one law for you; and ye have agreed together to speak before me lying and corrupt words, till the time be changed; only tell me the dream, and I shall know that ye can declare unto me the interpretation thereof.'

10 The Chaldeans answered before the king, and said: 'There is not a man up-on the earth that can declare the king's matter; forasmuch as no great and powerful king hath asked such a thing of any magician, or enchanter, or Chaldean. 11 And it is a hard thing that the king asketh, and there is none other that can declare it before the king, except the G-ds, whose dwelling is not with flesh.'

12 For this cause the king was angry and very furious, and commanded to destroy all the wise men of Babylon. 13 So the decree went forth, and the wise men were to be slain; and they sought Daniel and his companions to be slain.

This is the introduction to the scene in which Daniel found himself. Included within this group of wise men, should they fail, he would also be killed. Verses 14-16:

> 14 Then Daniel returned answer with counsel and discretion to Arioch the captain of the king's guard, who was gone forth to slay the wise men of Babylon; 15 he answered and said to Arioch the king's captain: 'Wherefore is the decree so peremptory from the king?' Then Arioch made the thing known to Daniel. 16 Then Daniel went in, and desired of the king that he would give him time, that he might declare unto the king the interpretation.

Daniel had faith in G-d and put that faith into action by fully depending on Him. He and his associates sought G-d for the solution. Verses 17-19:

> 17 Then Daniel went to his house, and made the thing known to Hananiah, Mishael, and Azariah, his companions; 18 that they might ask mercy of the G-d of heaven concerning this secret; that Daniel and his companions should not perish with the rest of the wise men of Babylon.
>
> 19 Then was the secret revealed unto

Daniel in a vision of the night. Then Daniel blessed the G-d of heaven.

Hear the words of praise that flowed from Daniel's lips since it was G-d Who provided the interpretation. Verses 20-23:

20 Daniel spoke and said: Blessed be the name of G-d From everlasting even unto everlasting; For wisdom and might are His; 21 And He changeth the times and the seasons; He removeth kings, and setteth up kings; He giveth wisdom unto the wise, And knowledge to them that know understanding;

22 He revealeth the deep and secret things; He knoweth what is in the darkness, And the light dwelleth with Him. 23 I thank Thee, and praise Thee, O Thou G-d of my fathers, Who hast given me wisdom and might, And hast now made known unto me what we desired of Thee; <u>For Thou hast made known unto us the king's matter.</u>

Daniel was brought before the king to interpret his dream. Verses 25-26:

25 Then Arioch brought in Daniel be-

fore the king in haste, and said thus unto him: 'I have found a man of the children of the captivity of Judah, that will make known unto the king the interpretation.'

26 The king spoke and said to Daniel, whose name was Belteshazzar: 'Art thou able to make known unto me the dream which I have seen, and the interpretation thereof?'

Daniel make known to the king the interpretation but he gave credit to G-d. Verses 27-30:

27 Daniel answered before the king, and said: 'The secret which the king hath asked can neither wise men, enchanters, magicians, nor astrologers, declare unto the king;

28 but there is a G-d in heaven that revealeth secrets, and He hath made known to the king Nebuchadnezzar what shall be in the end of days. Thy dream, and the visions of thy head upon thy bed, are these:

29 as for thee, O king, thy thoughts came [into thy mind] upon thy bed,

what should come to pass hereafter; and He that revealeth secrets hath made known to thee what shall come to pass.

30 But as for me, this secret is not revealed to me for any wisdom that I have more than any living, but to the intent that the interpretation may be made known to the king, and that thou mayest know the thoughts of thy heart.

Daniel first told the king the content of his dream and then he interpreted it for him. The content of the dream was known only to the king himself. Verses 31-36:

31 Thou, O king, sawest, and behold a great image. This image, which was mighty, and whose brightness was surpassing, stood before thee; and the appearance thereof was terrible [frightful].

32 As for that image, its head was of fine gold, its breast and its arms of silver, its belly and its thighs of brass, 33 its legs of iron, its feet part of iron and part of clay.

34 Thou sawest till that a stone was cut out without hands, which smote the image upon its feet that were of iron and clay, and broke them to pieces.

35 Then was the iron, the clay, the brass, the silver, and the gold, broken in pieces together, and became like the chaff of the summer threshing-floors; and the wind carried them away, so that no place was found for them; and the stone that smote the image became a great mountain, and filled the whole earth.

36 This is the dream; and we will tell the interpretation thereof before the king.

Before Daniel explains the great image to the king, he praises him. Think about the power this monarch wielded as king over other kings who ruled over other nations. That is important as this dream represents the future of these Gentile nations of whom this king is presently the head. Verses 37-38:

37 Thou, O king, king of kings, unto whom the G-d of heaven hath given the kingdom, the power, and the

strength, and the glory; 38 and wheresoever the children of men, the beasts of the field, and the fowls of the heaven dwell, hath He given them into thy hand, and hath made thee to rule over them all; thou art the head of gold.

Daniel continues with the kingdoms which will follow after him. Verses 39-43:

39 And after thee shall arise another kingdom inferior to thee; and another third kingdom of brass, which shall bear rule over all the earth. 40 And the fourth kingdom shall be strong as iron; forasmuch as iron breaketh in pieces and beateth down all things; and as iron that crusheth all these, shall it break in pieces and crush.

41 And whereas thou sawest the feet and toes, part of potters' clay, and part of iron, it shall be a divided kingdom; but there shall be in it of the firmness of the iron, forasmuch as thou sawest the iron mixed with miry clay.

42 And as the toes of the feet were part of iron, and part of clay, so part of the

kingdom shall be strong, and part thereof broken. 43 And whereas thou sawest the iron mixed with miry clay, they shall mingle themselves by the seed of men; but they shall not cleave [hold onto] one to another, even as iron doth not mingle with clay.

In this book, we are using a framework of seven days to understand Israel's history and future. The seven days of a week are meaningful because it ends with the eternal Shabbat. Therefore, the Gentiles are not given a day. G-d provides this explanation to benefit the Jews. The "time of the Gentiles" is illustrated in geopolitical stages because they are the multitude of "nations." Their timeframe begins with the reign of Nebuchadnezzar. The end of the "time of the Gentiles" will coincide with Israel's glorious destiny.

Daniel continues by speaking of another kingdom that G-d will set up. This will be the Davidic Kingdom. Verse 44:

44 And in the days of those kings shall the G-d of heaven set up a kingdom, which shall never be destroyed; nor shall the kingdom be left to another people; it shall break in pieces and consume all these kingdoms, but it

shall stand for ever.

There is no question that these verses refer to G-d's eternal plans and the destruction of the rebel nations. In the end, the King of Israel will be the Suzerain. All the other nations will be the Vassals.

In verse 44, Daniel speaks about something that will "break in pieces and consume all these kingdoms." Look at the following verses. We will see that the stone is cut from the mountain. What is this mountain? In the New Covenant, the mountain is Israel. Out of Israel comes a stone will be cut without hands or human intervention. Yeshua Ha-Mashiach specifically referred to this stone in Matthew 21.42:

> 42 [Yeshua] saith unto them, Did ye never read in the scriptures, <u>The stone which the builders rejected, the same is become the head of the corner</u>: this is the Lord's doing, and it is marvellous in our eyes?

To follow are the words King David spoke at the dedication of the Second Temple. (See Ezra 3.10-11.) Psalms 118.22:

> 22 <u>The stone which the builders rejected Is become the chief corner-stone.</u>

Notice what Yeshua HaMashiach or, figuratively speaking, the "stone" does to the nations that come against Israel! Daniel 2.45:

> 45 **Forasmuch as thou sawest <u>that a stone was cut out of the mountain without hands</u>, and that <u>it broke in pieces the iron, the brass, the clay, the silver, and the gold</u>; the great G-d hath made known to the king what shall come to pass hereafter; and the dream is certain, and the interpretation thereof sure.'**

Look at the response of this Gentile king to the words spoken to him by Daniel. King Nebuchadnezzar recognizes the unquestionable sovereignty of the G-d of Daniel – the G-d of Israel.

This great Gentile king who begins the "time of the Gentiles" acknowledged that the G-d of Israel is "the G-d of G-ds . . . the Lord of kings . . . and revealer of secrets" in verse 47:

> 47 **The king spoke unto Daniel, and said: 'Of a truth it is, that your G-d is the G-d of G-ds, and the Lord of kings, and a revealer of secrets, seeing thou hast been able to reveal this secret.'**

This statue is a composite of the many kingdoms of the "Time of the Gentiles." It used symbolism to explain something very complex. My goal is to provide you with a framework in which to view G-d's Word in its entirety.

Daniel explained the king that the golden head of the statue was Nebuchadnezzar himself. Later, an inferior kingdom would arise after Babylon. This is represented by the breast of silver. This would be the coalition of the kingdoms of Media and Persia which conquered Babylon at the time of Belshazzar. The breastplate of silver had two arms representing these two kingdoms. The belly of brass follows. It represents Alexander the Great who conquered the Medo-Persian kingdom and eventually subsumed into the Greek Empire. This included Babylon, parts of Asia, Egypt, Macedonia in Europe, and Syria. Alexander the Great built this Greek empire by uniting the East and the West into one.

The statue's legs were of made of iron. Following the fall of Alexander, the Greek empire was divided into four parts by his four generals who became overseers of his vast empire. This less unified empire was assimilated into the Roman Empire. They were known by their ruthless domination and subjugation of their citizens under "the iron foot of Rome." The toes on these feet were a composite of iron and clay. Towards its end, this may signify the fractionalization of the Roman Empire. Rome continues to represent the continuation of the Gentile's decentralized governments. Ultimately, over time, this will evolve into a centralized world government whose administration will, as with Rome, rule with an iron foot.

There is a book written by David Yonggi Cho. It was published in 1998 by Creation House Publishing in Lake Mary, Florida and entitled *The Apocalyptic Prophecy*. Cho deserves mention and not a footnote. This is an excellent example of one interpretation. We must not journey too far into the pucker brush. The key takeaway from this chapter in Daniel 2 is that we can now establish two comparative timeframes. We have two timeframes: one for the Jews and one for the Gentiles. This is the point! We can put them side-by-side because they both end up at the same place and the same time.

These last two chapters gave a lot to take in. Let us step back for just a moment. So, there are two timeframes. Each one has its own destiny, but they run concurrently. They both arrive at the end at the same time. This will occur at the end of seven remaining years spoken about in Daniel 9. Yeshua confirms this in Matthew 24. Paul, the Apostle to the Gentiles, explained to the Gentiles what was happening to Israel so they could also understand.

At the end of the following verse, there is another time reference for us. It tells us when the Age of the Gentiles will end. Romans 11.25:

> **25 For I would not, [Gentile] brethren, that ye should be ignorant of this mystery, lest ye should be wise in your own conceits; that blindness in part is happened to Israel, <u>until the fulness of the Gentiles be come in.</u>**

As Paul continues, we find a bonus. This Gentile Apostle acknowledges the certain fulfillment of the covenant G-d made with Israel. Verses 26-27:

> **26 And <u>so [then] all Israel shall be saved</u>: as it is written, There shall come out of Sion the Deliverer, and shall turn away ungodliness from Jacob: 27 <u>For this is my covenant unto them [Israel], when I shall take away their sins.</u>**

It is important to remember that true and faithful Israel will be victorious. Why? It is because G-d promised it. The victory will apply to only those who believe and continue to trust in the Word of G-d!

18

Two Or More Witnesses

The Mosaic Law requires two or three witnesses (Deut. 17.6). A man cannot be convicted and put to death based upon hearsay. Eyewitnesses must provide credible testimony. The word "testimony" means "a solemn declaration or affirmation made for the purpose of establishing or proving the facts." Testimonies come from the personal observations of these eyewitnesses. Each of the first four books of the New Covenant is an eyewitness's account called a "gospel" meaning "good news." These four books are personal testimonies written by individuals who were with HaMashiach throughout His ministry. These eyewitness accounts were inspired by G-d and include the words and actions of Yeshua HaMashiach during His life.

It is important for us to look again at two Scriptures. Below is the prophecy concerning the New Covenant recorded in Jeremiah 31.31-32:

31 Behold, the days come, saith the LORD, that <u>I will make a new covenant with the house of Israel, and with the house of Judah;</u>

32 not according to the covenant that I made with their fathers in the day that I took them by the hand to bring them out of the land of Egypt; forasmuch as they broke My covenant, although I was a lord over them, saith the LORD.

Pay attention to the following and you will see the fulfillment of Daniel's prophecy. Verses 33-34:

33 But this is the covenant that I will make with the house of Israel after those days, saith the LORD, <u>I will put My law in their inward parts, and in their heart will I write it; and I will be their G-d, and they shall be My people;</u>

34 and they shall teach no more every man his neighbour, and every man his brother, saying: 'Know the LORD'; for they shall all know Me, from the least of them unto the greatest of them, saith the LORD; <u>for I will forgive their iniquity, and their sin will I remember no more.</u>

When will this New Covenant be fulfilled? Look again at the prophecy G-d gave to Daniel:

> (1) to finish the transgression, and to make an end of sin,
> (2) to forgive iniquity, and to bring in everlasting righteousness,
> (3) to seal vision and prophet, and
> (4) to anoint the most holy place.

This New Covenant will be fulfilled at the end of seven years. Until then, Israel must not lose hope.

Archaeologists lay out various pieces as they discover them. This is like a puzzle. We are putting together the pieces and, gradually, a picture begins to appear. Take this idea of puzzle pieces and think about this verse from Isaiah. He asked G-d how he should teach the people so that they would understand. Here is G-d's response to him. Isaiah 28.9-11:

> 9 **Whom shall one teach knowledge? And whom shall one make to understand the message? Them that are weaned from the milk, Them that are drawn from the breasts?**
>
> 10 **For it is precept by precept, precept by precept, Line by line, line by line; Here a little, there a little.**

11 For with stammering lips and with a strange tongue Shall it be spoken to this people;

Be patient as we work through this presentation as I provide you with evidence to consider. Be patient. You need all the evidence to come to an informed verdict. I promise you that all the pieces of the puzzle will soon fit together into the complete picture.

There is no way to accomplish something without pressing on. The children of Israel were at the sea. Looking over their shoulders, they saw the Egyptian army in hot pursuit. They had faith and pressed on. The new holy nation of Israel were encamped on the Jordan River. They looked over to the other side and saw the Promised Land. They had faith and pressed on. Compare those situations with our present position. We are standing on the shore of the Old Covenant and looking over at the New Covenant promised to Israel. We must have faith and press on.

You have most likely been taught that the books of the New Covenant or New Testament belongs to the Christians. This is absolutely not true! G-d is very clear to whom He was speaking, "I will make a new covenant with the house of Israel, and with the house of Judah" (Jer. 31:31). Yet, many Christian churches teach Replacement Theology.

188

They teach that the promises made to Israel were transferred to the Church. That is a lie. G-d does not change and this especially applies to an unconditional promise. I will provide it! Consider the title of this book: *The Glorious Destiny of Israel: The Fulfillment of G-d's Promises and Prophecies to Israel.* Their promises and prophecies were given to them by G-d. Believing G-d's Word, we must press on.

The New Covenant begins with the written testimonies of four eyewitnesses. The word "gospel" means "good news." Since these four books were written to Jews, we can assume that the "good news" is for the sons and daughters of Abraham. Each individual's account provides historical facts about the earthly ministry of Yeshua HaMashiach presented from their own perspective. G-d's promises He made to Abraham, Isaac, Jacob, and King David were coming true. The "good new" is for their children.

The Apostle Paul, a Pharisee who studied under Gamaliel, explained something to the Gentiles. I am going to show you something that most Christians today miss completely. Paul told them that the purpose of Yeshua's earthly ministry was "to fulfill the promises made to the fathers." Romans 15.8:

8 Now I say that [Yeshua HaMashiach] was a minister <u>of the circumcision</u> for the truth of G-d, <u>to confirm the promises made unto the fathers</u>:

Here we have the words of Paul, the Apostle to the Gentiles, who made this bold statement. The word "circumcision" refers directly to "the Jews." So, HaMashiach came to fulfill the promises made to Abraham, Isaac, Jacob, Moses, and King David.

Replacement Theology teaches that the covenants G-d made with Israel were transferred to the Church. As I said before, this is a false and is contrary to Scripture. Here is a brief story. I was having lunch with some Christians one of whom held to this belief. I asked him if he believed in the covenant of marriage. He was shocked with a sort of righteous indignation that I would ask such a question. After he said that he did, I continued, "Let me ask you another question. Is your covenant transferrable?" He was sitting with his lovely wife and was appalled. He firmly asserted, "Covenants cannot be transferred!" Smiling, I told him perhaps he should think about that. G-d's covenants are non-transferrable . . . period.

Back to Daniel's prophecy, the kingdom will be established and the Anointed One, a descendant of King David, will sit upon David's throne forever.

This will occur at the end of Daniel's 490 years. Wait a minute. How will anyone know if David's heir is legitimate or not? We would need proof that this Heir is legitimately as descendant of Abraham as well as King David. This would be of primary interest to the Jews. There must be a record documenting the legitimacy of the Heir.

Let us look at the very first verse of the very first book of the New Covenant. Matthew 1.1:

> **1 The book of the generation of [Yeshua HaMashiach], the son of David, the son of Abraham.**

Matthew begins by providing the detailed genealogy of Yeshua HaMashiach beginning with Abraham. The genealogy ends with this summary in verse 1.17:

> **17 So all the generations from Abraham to David are fourteen generations; and from David until the carrying away into Babylon are fourteen generations; and from the carrying away into Babylon unto [HaMashiach] are fourteen generations.**

The Gospel of Luke also includes a geneaology. This one begins with Joseph and goes backwards to Adam. In both genealogies, King David is included. Their purpose was to establish that Yeshua is a direct descendant of King David. Matthew established the legitimacy of Yeshua to the title Son of David. Luke established the title Son of Man. These two titles are used repeatedly throughout the Gospels.

The first five books of the New Covenant are important for Jews to understand for they are a continuation of the Old Covenant. Notice that HaMashiach taught Jewish believers exclusively. During His earthly ministry, He excluded the Gentiles. When He was sending out His Twelve, He gave instructions. They were bringing the "good new" of the Kingdom to "the lost sheep of the house of Israel." Matthew 10.5-6:

> 5 **These twelve [Yeshua] sent forth, and commanded them, saying, 'Go not into the way of the Gentiles, and into any city of the Samaritans enter ye not:**
>
> 6 **But go rather to the lost sheep of the house of Israel.'**

Like Moses and David who were shepherds, so too was Yeshua HaMashiach a shepherd of Israel.

You may see the word "Greeks" used in the

New Covenant. They are the "Gentiles" or "non-Jews." The Greeks based their lives on philosophy – the knowledge or science of man while the Jews based their lives on the wisdom of G-d. Here is an incident where some Greeks who had heard of HaMashiach came to see Him. However, Yeshua chose to ignore them. John 12.20-23:

> 20 **And there were certain Greeks among them that came up to worship at the feast:** 21 **The same came therefore to Philip, which was of Bethsaida of Galilee, and desired him, saying, Sir, we would [desire to] see [Yeshua].**

> 22 **Philip cometh and telleth Andrew: and again Andrew and Philip tell [Yeshua].** 23 **And [Yeshua] answered them, saying, The hour is come, that the Son of man should be glorified.**

He ignored the request of the Gentiles saying, "The hour is come, that the Son of man should be glorified." During His earthly ministry, HaMashiach would minister exclusively to "the lost sheep of the house of Israel."

19

Good News Of The Kingdom

Where are we on Daniel's timeline? The prophecy stated that will be seven years remaining after the Anointed One is cut off. Yeshua, the Shepherd, is present with His sheep for three years. So, at the beginning of His ministry, there would be ten years before the establishment of David's kingdom. What was the message Yeshua delivered? Matthew 4.23:

> 23 And [Yeshua] went about all Galilee, teaching in their synagogues, and preaching <u>the gospel of the kingdom</u>, and healing all manner of sickness and all manner of disease among the people.

We were told by the Apostle Paul that Yeshua came to confirm "the promises made to the fathers."

We can confirm that His message was to proclaim the good news of the kingdom which the Jews earnestly sought. The Davidic Kingdom was the eternal kingdom promised to King David. There was an Old Covenant prophet by the name of John the Baptist. The Prophet Isaiah foretold about this herald who would proclaim the arrival of Ha-Mashiach. Matthew 3.1-3:

> 1 **In those days came John the Baptist, preaching in the wilderness of Judaea,**
> 2 **And saying, Repent ye: <u>for the kingdom of heaven is at hand.</u>**
>
> 3 **For this is he that was spoken of by the prophet Esaias [Isaiah], saying, The voice of one crying in the wilderness, <u>Prepare ye the way of the Lord, make his paths straight.</u>**

Yeshua HaMashiach started His ministry when He was thirty years old. As was the custom, He was baptized. Following His baptism by John the Baptist, He was led into the wilderness to be tested for forty days. Then, He traveled to His hometown of Nazareth to make a public proclamation. Luke 4.16-21:

> 16 **And he [Yeshua] came to Nazareth, where he had been brought up: and, as**

is custom was, he went into the synagogue on the sabbath day, and stood
up for to read. 17 And there was delivered unto him the book of the prophet
Esaias. And when he had opened the
book, he found the place where it was
written,

18 The Spirit of the Lord is upon me,
because he hath anointed me to preach
the gospel to the poor; he hath sent me
to heal the brokenhearted, to preach
deliverance to the captives, and recov-
ering of sight to the blind, to set at lib-
erty them that are bruised, 19 To preach
the acceptable year of the Lord.

20 And he closed the book, and he gave
it again to the minister, and sat down.
And the eyes of all them that were in
the synagogue were fastened on him. 21
And he began to say unto them, This
day is this scripture fulfilled in your
ears.

Why were all eyes *fastened on Him* as He returned to
His seat? The Jews knew their Scripture and He had
stopped reading Isaiah in the middle of a verse! Before He sat down, He proclaimed that this portion
of Scripture had been "fulfilled in their hearing."

Let us take a look at the two portions of this Scripture. Isaiah 61.1-2:

> 1 **The spirit of the Lord G-d is upon me [HaMashiach]; Because the LORD hath anointed me [HaMashiach] To bring good tidings unto the humble; He hath sent me to bind up the broken-hearted, To proclaim liberty to the captives, And the opening of the eyes to them that are bound;**
>
> 2 **To proclaim the year of the LORD'S good pleasure . . .**

There, He stopped. He did not finish verse 2 and returned the scroll to the attendant before going to sit down. Why?

The reason has to do with a separation of time. Here is the remainder of verse 2:

> 2 **. . . And the day of vengeance of our G-d;**

Yeshua HaMashiach had stopped mid-verse because "the day of vengeance" or the Tribulation would not begin until after His death. The people of the "prince" who will not appear until after the Anointed One is cutoff. While He was with His

198

brethren, He is "to bring good tidings" by proclaiming "the good news of the Kingdom."

While He was with them, that is what He did. Matthew 4.23:

> 23 And [Yeshua] went about all Galilee, teaching in their synagogues, and preaching <u>the gospel of the kingdom,</u> and healing all manner of sickness and all manner of disease among the people.

Yeshua's miracles are His credentials. Our highlights of the four gospels is just that. At your leisure, consider reading the four gospels. There is a lot of detail provided concerning HaMashiach. Compare the events recorded in the gospels with those prophesied in the Tanakh. See if it makes sense using G-d's seven days of Creation's Restoration.

Here is an example. This event occurred at the beginning of the week in which Yeshua Mashiach was crucified. Matthew verses 21.6-9:

> 6 And the disciples went, and did as [Yeshua] commanded them, 7 And brought the ass, and the colt, and put on them their clothes, and they set him [Yeshua] thereon.

8 And a very great multitude spread their garments in the way; others cut down branches from the trees, and strawed them in the way.

9 And the multitudes that went before, and that followed, cried, saying, <u>Hosanna to the Son of David: Blessed is he that cometh in the name of the Lord; Hosanna in the highest.</u>

This event fulfilled the prophecy in Zechariah 9.9:

9 Rejoice greatly, O daughter of Zion, Shout, O daughter of Jerusalem; <u>Behold, thy king cometh unto thee, He is triumphant, and victorious, Lowly, and riding upon an ass, Even upon a colt the foal of an ass.</u>

His reception by the rulers of Israel was quite the opposite. Yeshua expressed His feelings to His disciples in Matthew 23.36-39:

36 Verily I say unto you, All these things shall come upon this generation.

37 O Jerusalem, Jerusalem, thou that killest the prophets, and stonest them which are sent unto thee, how often

**would I have gathered thy children to-
gether, even as a hen gathereth her
chickens under her wings, and ye
would not!**

**38 Behold, your house is left unto you
desolate. 39 For I say unto you, Ye shall
not see me henceforth, till ye shall say,
<u>Blessed is he that cometh in the name
of the Lord</u>.**

Those last words are the ones Israel must cry out
before He will return to save them.

Later, the Twelve made remarks about the
beauty of the temple at sunset. Yeshua remarks to
them about its future. Matthew 24.1-2:

**1 And [Yeshua] went out, and departed
from the temple: and his disciples
came to him for to shew him the build-
ings of the temple.**

**2 And [Yeshua] said unto them, See ye
not all these things? verily I say unto
you, There shall not be left here one
stone upon another, that shall not be
thrown down.**

The entire chapter of Matthew 24 is about the end

times. For our purpose, we will include this chapter completely. Now, alone with His Twelve, look at the questions they ask Yeshua in private. Verse 3:

> 3 And as he [Yeshua] sat upon the mount of Olives, the disciples came unto him privately, saying, <u>Tell us, when shall these things be? and what shall be the sign of thy coming, and of the end of the world?</u>

Now, we must pay close attention. His answer will tie into Daniel's prophecy that we studied earlier. His response begins in verses 4-7:

> 4 And [Yeshua] answered and said unto them, <u>Take heed that no man deceive you</u>. 5 For many shall come in my name, saying, I am Christ; and shall deceive many.
>
> 6 And ye shall hear of wars and rumours of wars: see that ye be not troubled: for all these things must come to pass, but the end is not yet.
>
> 7 For nation shall rise against nation, and kingdom against kingdom: and there shall be famines, and pestilences, and earthquakes, in divers places.

The seven remaining years of Daniel's 490 years are still, as of this writing, in abeyance. I say abeyance because something happened. Certainly, by now, it would have been completed, right? We will get to the cause of that suspension later. But, for now, Yeshua's response to their question concerns the "seven last years" called the Tribulation. The Prophet Jeremiah called them, Jacob's "time of trouble" in Jeremiah 30.7:

> 7 **Alas! for that day is great, So that none is like it; And it is a time of trouble unto Jacob, But out of it shall he [Jacob now Israel] be saved.**

Did you notice how it ends? Jacob, now Israel, will be saved!

Yeshua continued to speak of the future. Note that this specifically applies "to the sons and daughters of Abraham." Matthew 24:8-12:

> 8 **All these are <u>the beginning of sorrows</u>. 9 Then <u>shall they deliver you up to be afflicted</u>, and <u>shall kill you</u>: and ye <u>shall be hated of all nations</u> for my name's sake.**
>
> 10 **And then <u>shall many be offended</u>, and <u>shall betray one another</u>, and <u>shall</u>**

hate one another. 11 And many false prophets shall rise, and **shall deceive many.**

12 And because **iniquity shall abound,** the **love of many shall wax cold.** 13 But he that shall endure unto the end, the same shall be saved.

Notice the last verse. Those who "endure unto the end" are true Israel and, as such, they will be saved!

In the following verse, Yeshua speaks about a specific gospel which He refers to as "this gospel of the kingdom." Remember, the word "gospel" means "good news." This gospel is the same good news preached by Yeshua and His Twelve during His earthly ministry. He states that, in the end times, this same gospel, the Gospel of the Kingdom, will be preached. Remember, the "end times" are the last seven years of the 490 years! Verse 14:

14 And **this gospel of the kingdom** shall be preached in all the world for a witness unto all nations; and then shall the end come.

This same message will be preached to all nations and, then, the end shall come. He is speaking about the last seven years still to come.

Yeshua referred to Daniel in verse 15:

15 When ye therefore shall <u>see the</u> <u>abomination of desolation</u>, <u>spoken of</u> <u>by Daniel the prophet</u>, stand in the ho-ly place, (whoso readeth, let him un-derstand:)

There are two different names for the same thing. One uses the "abomination of desolation" while the other uses "appalment." Let again at Daniel 9.27:

27 And he shall make a firm covenant with many for one week; and for half of the week he shall cause the sacrifice and the offering to cease; and upon the wing of <u>detestable things shall be that</u> <u>which causeth appalment</u>; and that un-til the extermination wholly deter-mined be poured out upon <u>that which</u> <u>causeth appalment</u>.'

Next, Yeshua offered a warning to any who will listen to the Word of G-d. This applies as much today as it did the day He said it to His Twelve. Matthew 24:16-20:

16 Then let them which be in Judaea flee into the mountains: 17 Let him which is on the housetop not come

down to take any thing out of his house:

18 Neither let him which is in the field return back to take his clothes. 19 And woe unto them that are with child, and to them that give suck in those days!

20 But pray ye that your flight be not in the winter, neither on the sabbath day:

The seven-year tribulation is divided into two parts. The covenant or peace treaty will be signed allowing Israel to rebuild their temple and restart the sacrifices. Halfway through the seven-year covenant, this "prince" enters the temple, stops the sacrifices, and perform some act referred to as "the abomination of desolation." This event marks the midpoint and, from here, things get really bad. This "prince" knows from prophecy his days are numbers and, therefore, the tribulation increases in its intensity until the end.

Do not be concerned! Victory has been promised. We have G-d's Word on this. Look again at Jeremiah 30.4-7:

4 And these are the words that the LORD spoke <u>concerning Israel and concerning Judah</u>. 5 For thus saith the

LORD: We have heard a voice of trembling, Of fear, and not of peace.

6 Ask ye now, and see whether a man doth travail with child; Wherefore do I see every man With his hands on his loins, as a woman in travail, And all faces are turned into paleness?

7 Alas! for <u>that day is great</u>, <u>So that none is like it; And it is a time of trouble unto Jacob, But out of it shall he be saved.</u>

Fear may become unbearable, but Jacob will be saved. May the G-d of Israel be praised!

Let us go back to Matthew 24 where Yeshua is speaking about the final three and one-half years of the Tribulation. Verses 24.21-28:

21 For then shall be <u>great tribulation,</u> such as was not since the beginning of the world to this time, no, nor ever shall be. 22 And except those days should be shortened, there should no flesh be saved: but for the elect's sake those days shall be shortened.

23 Then if any man shall say unto you,

Lo, here is [HaMashiach], or there; believe it not. 24 For there shall arise false messiahs, and false prophets, and shall shew great signs and wonders; insomuch that, if it were possible, they shall deceive the very elect.

25 Behold, I have told you before. 26 Wherefore if they shall say unto you, Behold, he is in the desert; go not forth: behold, he is in the secret chambers; believe it not.

27 For as the lightning cometh out of the east, and shineth even unto the west; so shall also the coming of the Son of man be.

28 For wheresoever the carcase [carcass or dead body] is, there will the eagles be gathered together.

Yeshua spoke about false prophets – those who preach contrary to G-d's word. He tells the children of Abraham not to be fooled. Again, anything contrary to Scripture . . . is from the deceiver.

He disclosed the end of the seven years. All of the nations will focus their energies and strength on accomplishing one thing: destroying G-d's people.

At that point, HaMashiach will return to defend Israel and destroy their enemies. Verses 29-31:

> 29 Immediately after the tribulation of those days shall the sun be darkened, and the moon shall not give her light, and the stars shall fall from heaven, and the powers of the heavens shall be shaken:

> 30 And then shall appear the sign of the Son of man in heaven: and then shall all the tribes [nations] of the earth mourn, and they shall see the Son of man coming in the clouds of heaven with power and great glory.

> 31 And he shall send his angels with a great sound of a trumpet, and they shall gather together his elect [Israel] from the four winds, from one end of heaven to the other.

Yeshua used an analogy to explain the signs of His Coming in verses 32-35:

> 32 Now learn [from] a parable of the fig tree; When his branch is yet tender, and putteth forth leaves, ye know that summer is nigh:

33 So likewise ye, when ye shall see all these things, know that it is near, even at the doors.

34 Verily I say unto you, This generation [that sees this] shall not pass, till all these things be fulfilled.

35 <u>Heaven and earth shall pass away, but my words shall not pass away.</u>

When will all this happen? Here is His answer to the disciples' original questions: "When shall these things be?" and "What shall be the sign of thy coming, and of the end of the world?" Verses 36-39:

36 But of that day and hour knoweth no man, no, not the angels of heaven, but my Father only. 37 But as the days of Noe [Noah] were, so shall also the coming of the Son of man be.

38 For as in the days that were before the flood they were eating and drinking, marrying and giving in marriage, until the day that Noe entered into the ark, 39 And knew not until the flood came, and took them all away; so shall also the coming of the Son of man be.

This Coming will be sudden and unexpected except for those who have watched for the signs.

The following two verses are often misinterpreted by Christians. They believe it refers to the Rapture, but it does not. This is all about Israel! It refers to the taking away of those who are not worthy. Those who remain will be the true sons or daughters of Abraham. We have discussed the importance of "faith" in G-d's Word. Those who endure unto the end will enter the kingdom. Verses 40-41:

> 40 **Then shall two be in the field; the one shall be taken, and the other left.** 41 **Two women shall be grinding at the mill; the one shall be taken, and the other left.**

Yeshua ends with a charge to remain vigilant. They are the ones who will remain after His resurrection to teach true Israel. Verses 42-51:

> 42 **Watch therefore: for ye know not what hour your Lord doth come.** 43 **But know this, that if the goodman of the house had known in what watch the thief would come, he would have watched, and would not have suffered**

his house to be broken up.

44 Therefore be ye also ready: for in such an hour as ye think not the Son of man cometh. 45 Who then is a faithful and wise servant, whom his lord hath made ruler over his household, to give them meat in due season?

46 Blessed is that servant, whom his lord when he cometh shall find so doing. 47 Verily I say unto you, That he shall make him ruler over all his goods.

48 But and if that evil servant shall say in his heart, My lord delayeth his coming; 49 And shall begin to smite his fellowservants, and to eat and drink with the drunken;

50 The lord of that servant shall come in a day when he looketh not for him, and in an hour that he is not aware of, 51 And shall cut him asunder, and appoint him his portion with the hypocrites: there shall be weeping and gnashing of teeth.

Matthew 24 is the one chapter in the gospels

dedicated to the last seven years of Daniel's 490-year prophecy. Later, it will be confirmed again in the books called "the Hebrew epistles." The word "epistle" simply means "letter." We will look at these epistles shortly. We are progressing nicely. For those who have persevered thus far, I make you this promise. Your investment of time will be worth it.

Let us end this chapter with some wonderful news for the true sons and daughters of Abraham. Like him, they have "faith in G-d's Word." The LORD spoke about these faithful in Jeremiah 24.6-7:

> 6 And <u>I will</u> <u>set Mine eyes upon them</u> for good, and <u>I will bring them back to this land</u>; and <u>I will build them</u>, and not pull them down; and <u>I will plant them</u>, and not pluck them up.
>
> 7 And <u>I will give them a heart to know Me</u>, that I am the LORD; and <u>they shall be My people</u>, and I will be their G-d; <u>for they shall return unto Me with their whole heart.</u>

There is indeed good news! These prophecies are as solid as a Rock. They are firm and unchanging. They will be fulfilled because the LORD G-d of Israel has said so. True Israel believes in G-d's Word.

They hold fast to their faith in Him!

20

Parables

The word "parable" comes from the Greek verb meaning "to compare." A story is used to teach the people a lesson. It compares two thing, one of which they are familiar. This method was used by Yeshua when teaching the Jews. There are over thirty parables recorded in the gospels each teaching the deep truths of G-d. We are going to select one that has to do with the land promised to Abraham and his seed. This particular parable appears three times in the gospels: Matthew 21.33-46, Mark 12.1-12, and Luke 20.9-18. Mark 12.1-2:

> 1 And he began to speak unto them by parables. A certain man planted a vineyard, and set an hedge about it, and digged a place for the winefat, and built a tower, and let [leased] it out to husbandmen, and went into a far country.

**2 And at the season he sent to the hus-
bandmen a servant, that he might receive from the husbandmen of the fruit
of the vineyard.**

The landowner rented his land out to tenants and
went away. After some time, the landowner sent a
servant to receive his portion of the produce. In
other words, he was to collect the rent due him. Let
us assume that the landlord would want ten percent
of the yield from the vineyard. How do these tenants respond to his representative? Verses 3-4:

**3 And they caught him, and beat him,
and sent him away empty. 4 And again
he sent unto them another servant; and
at him they cast stones, and wounded
him in the head, and sent him away
shamefully handled.**

They roughed him up and sent him back to
the landowner. The landowner was aware of this
shameful treatment. So, he sent additional representatives, one after another. Verse 5:

**5 And again he sent another; and him
they killed, and many others; beating
some, and killing some.**

No doubt this was a vast amount of land. He was

entitled to receive his dues. The landowner, having only one son, believed the tenants would respect him. Verses 6-8:

6 **Having yet therefore one son, his wellbeloved, he sent him also last unto them, saying, They will reverence my son.**

7 **But those husbandmen said among themselves, <u>This is the heir; come, let us kill him, and the inheritance shall be ours.</u>**

8 **And they took him, and killed him, and cast him out of the vineyard.**

This parable ends with the tenants killing the landowner's only son. Everyone listened with great interest to His stories. After presenting this case, He asks a question, "What shall the landlord of the vineyard do?" He tells them the answer in verse 9:

9 **What shall therefore the lord of the vineyard do? he will come and destroy the husbandmen, and will give the vineyard unto others.**

Imagine the crowd listening intently. There were some rulers of Israel present. Yeshua continued.

Verses 10-11:

> 10 **And have ye not read this scripture; The stone which the builders rejected is become the head of the corner:** 11 **This was the Lord's doing, and it is marvellous in our eyes?**

The corrupt rulers of Israel knew He was speaking against them. So, what was their reaction? Verse 12:

> 12 **And they sought to lay hold on him, but feared the people: for they knew that he had spoken the parable against them: and they left him, and went their way.**

It was not long after this that Yeshua Ha-Mashiach was executed by crucifixion. Soon the Anointed One would be "cut off." Compare this to Jeremiah 11.19:

> 19 **But I was like a docile lamb that is led to the slaughter; And I knew not that they had devised devices against me: 'Let us destroy the tree with the fruit thereof, <u>And let us cut him off from the land of the living, That his name may be no more remembered.</u>'**

The killing of Yeshua HaMashiach Who is the Lamb of G-d would be the pivotal event. According to Daniel's prophecy, it would initiate the remaining seven years. This event of the Anointed One being "cut off" also coincides with the appearance of the "prince" who is called the Antichrist. Along with him comes a flood of people who will seek to destroy Jerusalem, its temple, and G-d's people.

However, something happened. Something caused G-d to declare a "temporary suspension" of Daniel's final seven years. Like a good cliffhanger, we will end this chapter here and continue this in the next.

21

The New Covenant

The New Covenant was promised in Jeremiah 31. It was introduced by Yeshua HaMashiach during His last Passover meal with His Twelve that occurred the night before He was crucified. Passover memorializes the night the LORD saved Israel. It concerns the last miracle to secure the release of Israel from Egyptian captivity: death of all first born. However, by marking their doorways with the blood of a lamb, the angel of death would "pass over" the homes of faithful Israel and leave them unaffected.

The Passover Lamb must be spotless and without blemish. For three years the Lamb would live among His brethren ministering to them. At the start of that ministry, look at what John the Baptist said concerning Yeshua HaMashiach before His baptism. John 1.29:

29 The next day John seeth [Yeshua] coming unto him, and saith, <u>Behold the Lamb of G-d</u>, which taketh away the sin of the world.

Look at the prophecy concerning the Lamb in Isaiah 53.7-8:

7 He was oppressed, and he was afflicted, yet he opened not his mouth: <u>he is brought as a lamb to the slaughter, and as a sheep before her shearers is dumb</u>, so he openeth not his mouth.

8 He was taken from prison and from judgment: and who shall declare his generation? for <u>he was cut off</u> out of the land of the living: <u>for the transgression of my people was he stricken</u>.

Let us join the last Passover with HaMashiach and His disciples the night before His crucifixion. Matthew 26.17-20:

17 Now the first day of the feast of unleavened bread the disciples came to [Yeshua], saying unto him, Where wilt thou that we prepare for thee to eat the passover? 18 And he said, Go into the city to such a man, and say unto him,

the Master saith, My time is at hand; I will keep the passover at thy house with my disciples.

19 And the disciples did as [Yeshua] had appointed them; and they made ready the passover. 20 Now when the even [evening] was come, he sat down with the twelve.

These Twelve that Yeshua had been during His three-year ministry, He would share His last meal with them. The narrative tells of this Passover Seder. Verses 26-29:

26 And as they were eating, [Yeshua] took bread, and blessed it, and brake it, and gave it to the disciples, and said, Take, eat; this is my body. 27 And he took the cup, and gave thanks, and gave it to them, saying, Drink ye all of it;

28 For this is my blood of the [New Covenant], which is shed for many for the remission of sins. 29 But I say unto you, I will not drink henceforth of this fruit of the vine, until that day when I drink it new with you in my Father's kingdom.

In less than twenty-four hours, He would be arrested, tried, convicted, sentenced, and executed.

Let us pause for a moment and reflect on this. There is much symbolism in the Passover Seder. Those who are personally familiar with it can take time to consider their meaning. The next day would be the point in time when the Anointed One would be "cut off." We would then expect the final seven years to begin leading up to the destruction of the nations "that come against Jerusalem." Zechariah 12.9-10:

> 9 **And it shall come to pass in that day, That I will seek to destroy all the nations That come against Jerusalem.**
>
> 10 **And I will pour upon the house of David, And upon the inhabitants of Jerusalem, The spirit of grace and of supplication; And they shall look unto Me because they have thrust him through; And they shall mourn for him, as one mourneth <u>for his only son</u>, And shall be in bitterness for him, as one that is in bitterness for <u>his firstborn</u>.**

What was the purpose of HaMashiach dying? He was to fulfill the Law. Yeshua made this clear in

Matthew 5.17-18

17 **Think not that I am come to destroy the law, or the prophets: <u>I am not come to destroy, but to fulfil.</u>**

18 **For verily I say unto you, <u>Till heaven and earth pass, one jot or one tittle shall in no wise pass from the law, till all be fulfilled.</u>**

The life of HaMashiach was recorded in the four of the gospels. I recommend you consider reading the Gospel of Matthew first. You can read the details surrounding His life, earthly ministry, trial, death, burial, and resurrection. All of this was done to meet the requirements of the Law and fulfill what was spoken about Him by the prophets.

Your independent study will lead to a deeper understanding. As you read, think about the framework we are presenting. HaMashiach came for "the lost sheep of the house of Israel." He came "to fulfill the promises made to the fathers." Finally He came to fulfill the requirements of the Law. We are still on the Fifth Day which is the Day of Law. The Law has never changed. The Mosaic Covenant is still in force. Its conditions remain the same. G-d requires perfect obedience to the Law. Consider this. What if the LORD Himself fulfilled all the requirements of the Law? What if He did it on behalf of Israel? This is referred to as "substitutionary atonement." It means that someone else pays the debts of someone else. How can this be? This is the benefit of the New Covenant which was revealed by Yeshia at the Passover Seder. Jeremiah 31.33-34:

> **33 But this is the [new] covenant that I will make with the house of Israel after those days, saith the LORD, I will put My law in their inward parts, and in their heart will I write it; and I will be their G-d, and they shall be My people;**

> **34 and they shall teach no more every man his neighbour, and every man his brother, saying: 'Know the LORD'; for <u>they shall all know Me</u>, from the least of them unto the greatest of them, saith the LORD; <u>for I will forgive their iniquity, and their sin will I remember no more.</u>**

Through the New Covenant the requirements of the Law were fulfilled. It is His righteousness before the Law that Yeshua HaMashiach accomplished. He was, is, and will be the spotless Lamb of G-d. At the end of the seven years, something amazing will happen. Because of Yeshua HaMashiach, the Lamb of G-d, Israel's iniquity can be forgiven and their sins remembered no more.

22

The Big Fish Story

This story is really about a test of faith. Not only was it a test of faith for the main character in the story, but also for some readers to believe it. It is a story about what G-d wanted and what a religious zealot did to thwart G-d from doing it. This story is about a prophet named Jonah who is mentioned in 2 Kings 14.25:

> **25 . . . according to the word of the LORD, the G-d of Israel, which He spoke by the hand of His servant Jonah . . . the prophet . . .**

This provides evidence that Jonah was both a real person and a prophet of G-d. Although the story of Jonah and the big fish is viewed by most as a fable, it will serve G-d's purpose.

Here is the beginning of the story. Jonah 1.1-3:

1 Now <u>the word of the LORD came unto Jonah</u> the son of Amittai, saying: **2**
'Arise, <u>go to Nineveh,</u> that great city,
<u>and proclaim against it;</u> for their wick-
edness is come up before Me.'

3 <u>But Jonah rose up to flee</u> unto Tarshish <u>from the presence of the LORD;</u>
and he went down to Joppa, and found
a ship going to Tarshish; so he paid the
fare thereof, and went down into it, to
go with them unto Tarshish, [away]
from the presence of the LORD

The problem with Ninevah was it was the capital of
a heathen nation of Gentiles. Therefore, when Jonah
the prophet received instructions from G-d, he pur-
posely sailed away from where G-d told him to go.
Most bosses would have pink-slipped this prophet,
but G-d had a far greater purpose. It would be a
message G-d sent to past, present, and future Jews.
We are going to focus on Noah.

A great storm came upon the boat. It was so
severe that experienced seamen feared for their
lives. Verses 11-13:

11 Then said they unto him: 'What shall
we do unto thee, that the sea may be
calm unto us?' for the sea grew more

and more tempestuous. 12 And he said unto them: 'Take me up, and cast me forth into the sea; so shall the sea be calm unto you; for I know that for my sake this great tempest is upon you.'

13 Nevertheless the men rowed hard to bring it to the land; but they could not; for the sea grew more and more tempestuous against them.

So, Jonah was the cause. Verse 15-16:

15 So <u>they took up Jonah, and cast him forth into the sea; and the sea ceased from its raging.</u> 16 Then the men feared the LORD exceedingly; and they offered a sacrifice unto the LORD, and made vows.

There are those who accept and obey the LORD's word and those who reject and rebel against Him.

Jonah was saved from the sea and preserved in the belly of a great fish. Verse 2.1:

1 And the LORD prepared a great fish to swallow up Jonah; and Jonah was in the belly of the fish three days and three nights.

After this time, we are told that Jonah was released from the great fish. Verse 2.11:

> 11 And the LORD spoke unto the fish, and it vomited out Jonah upon the dry land.

Again, the LORD makes His instructions known. Verses 3.1-2:

> 1 And the word of the LORD came unto Jonah the second time, saying: 2 'Arise, go unto Nineveh, that great city, and make unto it the proclamation that I bid thee.'

Jonah responded. Verses 3.3-10:

> 3 So Jonah arose, and went unto Nineveh, according to the word of the LORD. Now Nineveh was an exceeding great city, of three days' journey. 4 And Jonah began to enter into the city a day's journey, and he proclaimed, and said: 'Yet forty days, and Nineveh shall be overthrown.'
>
> 5 And the people of Nineveh believed G-d; and they proclaimed a fast, and put on sackcloth, from the greatest of

them even to the least of them. 6 And the tidings reached the king of Nineveh, and he arose from his throne, and laid his robe from him, and covered him with sackcloth, and sat in ashes.

7 And he caused it to be proclaimed and published through Nineveh by the decree of the king and his nobles, saying: 'Let neither man nor beast, herd nor flock, taste any thing; let them not feed, nor drink water; 8 but let them be covered with sackcloth, both man and beast, and let them cry mightily unto G-d; yea, let them turn every one from his evil way, and from the violence that is in their hands.

9 Who knoweth whether G-d will not turn and repent, and turn away from His fierce anger, that we perish not?' 10 And G-d saw their works, that they turned from their evil way; and G-d repented of the evil, which He said He would do unto them; and He did it not.

This Gentile nation heard the message of the coming judgment Jonah delivered. They repented and turned from their evil ways.

We would think that Jonah would rejoice that, through his work, the LORD had accomplished His purpose. However, Jonah was angry and asked G-d to take his life. The story continues in verses 4.1-5:

1 But it displeased Jonah exceedingly, and he was angry. 2 And he prayed unto the LORD, and said: 'I pray Thee, O LORD, was not this my saying, when I was yet in mine own country? Therefore I fled beforehand unto Tarshish; for I knew that Thou art a gracious G-d, and compassionate, long-suffering, and abundant in mercy, and repentest Thee of the evil.

3 Therefore now, O LORD, take, I beseech Thee, my life from me; for it is better for me to die than to live.' 4 And the LORD said: 'Art thou greatly angry?' 5 Then Jonah went out of the city, and sat on the east side of the city, and there made him a booth, and sat under it in the shadow, till he might see what would become of the city.

Nineveh was a great city of the ancient Assyrian empire. It was a city of Gentiles. They were heathen, but G-d chose to show them mercy. Some Jews struggle with the idea that G-d would show mercy upon Gentiles. The reason I have included the story of Jonah will make sense shortly. The G-d of Israel is also the G-d of Creation. His will is sovereign over all – both the Jew and the non-Jew. Consider what G-d said to Moses in Exodus 33.19:

> 19 **And He said: 'I will make all My goodness pass before thee, and will proclaim the name of the LORD before thee; and <u>I will be gracious to whom I will be gracious, and will show mercy on whom I will show mercy</u>.'**

This statement, without qualifications, still stands.

Jonah was so angry. A gourd is a type of fruit and this plant appeared to provide shade for Jonah. It appeared and disappeared. Both were the result of G-d choosing to show mercy to Jonah and revoke that mercy. G-d provided examples of His sovereign will to Jonah – choosing to whom He will show mercy. Verses 6-11:

> 6 **And the LORD G-d prepared a gourd, and made it to come up over Jonah, <u>that it might be a shadow over his head</u>, to deliver him from his evil. So Jonah was exceeding glad because of the gourd. 7 But G-d prepared a worm when the morning rose the next day,**

and it smote the gourd, that it withered.

8 And it came to pass, when the sun arose, that G-d prepared a vehement east wind; and the sun beat upon the head of Jonah, that he fainted, and requested for himself that he might die, and said: 'It is better for me to die than to live.' 9 And G-d said to Jonah: 'Art thou greatly angry for the gourd?' And he said: 'I am greatly angry, even unto death.'

10 And the LORD said: 'Thou hast had pity on the gourd, for which thou hast not laboured, neither madest it grow, which came up in a night, and perished in a night; 11 and should not I have pity on Nineveh, that great city, wherein are more than sixscore thousand persons that cannot discern between their right hand and their left hand, and also much cattle?'

In Ninevah, that great city, there were more than 120,000 people who received G-d's mercy because He gave them the opportunity to repent. This is the point to remember going forward. The LORD is above all. He can choose to whom He will and will not show mercy for everything is His. This is His Creation.

There is one last piece of evidence that will add credibility to this story. It ties in completely with our purpose. Yeshua compared the Prophet Jonah to Himself. Matthew 12.38-41:

> **38 Then certain of the scribes and of the Pharisees answered, saying, Master, we would [wish to] see a sign from thee. 39 But he answered and said unto them, An evil and adulterous generation see-keth after a sign; and there shall no sign be given to it, but [except] <u>the sign of the prophet Jonas [Jonah]</u>:**
>
> **40 <u>For as Jonas was three days and three nights in the whale's belly; so shall the Son of man be three days and three nights in the heart of the earth.</u>**

Referring to those who would not repent and believe the Gospel of the Kingdom, Yeshua had these words for them. Verse 41:

> **41 The men of Nineveh shall rise in judgment with this generation, and shall condemn it: because they repent-ed at the preaching of Jonas; and, be-**

hold, a [Someone] greater than Jonas is here.

The rulers of that present day wanted a sign. Ha-Mashiach prophesied that the Son of Man would be three days and three nights in the heart of the earth. That means He would die. The gospels record that He was crucified, dead, and buried for three days. Then on the third day, G-d raised Him from the dead. Disbelief is the antithesis of faith. The Gentiles were given an opportunity to repent and they did. The lesson from this book is that G-d is sovereign and able to do His will by whatever means He chooses.

23

First Fruits

The Feast of Firstfruits or, as it is also called Shavuot or the Festival of Weeks, is one of Israel's holidays. Another name by which it is known is Pentecost because it begins seven weeks or fifty days after Passover. It marks the time when Israel begins its harvest and honors G-d with the presentation of the first fruits. Deuteronomy 16.9-10:

> 9 **Seven weeks shalt thou number unto thee; from the time [until] the sickle is first put to the standing corn shalt thou begin to number seven weeks.**

> 10 **And thou shalt keep the feast of weeks unto the LORD thy G-d after the measure of the freewill-offering of thy hand, which thou shalt give, according as the LORD thy G-d blesseth thee.**

All Jewish males were required to attend this celebration in Jerusalem. We will look at the first Pentecost following the resurrection of Yeshua HaMashiach. We will consider the application of First Fruits after some background is presented.

The good news of the Kingdom was preached to the Jews by HaMashiach and His Twelve throughout Israel for three years. If you read the four gospels, you will see the proclamation of the Kingdom Gospel preached repeatedly. Its message was about the coming of the Kingdom and, at that time, it was imminent. During His ministry there were two groups of Jews. There were those who had faith in Yeshua HaMashiach and believed what He preached. There were those who did not believe His message and rejected Him. As He went throughout Israel, He referred to those believers ready to enter the Kingdom as "the harvest." Matthew 9.36-38:

> 36 But when he saw the multitudes, he was moved with compassion on them, because they fainted, and were scattered abroad, as sheep having no shepherd.

> 37 Then saith he unto his disciples, <u>The harvest truly is plenteous, but the labourers are few;</u>

38 <u>Pray ye therefore the Lord of the harvest, that he will send forth labourers into his harvest.</u>

Jesus compared the harvest which is not due for another four month with the fields of spiritual believers ripe for harvest. John 4.35:

35 Say not ye, There are yet four months, and then cometh harvest? behold, I say unto you, Lift up your eyes, and look on the fields; for they are white already to harvest.

It was the first harvest of Kingdom Believers, those who believed and waited to receive the promised Spirit. This is the same Spirit of which David spoke in Psalm 51.12-14:

12 Create me a clean heart, O G-d; And renew a stedfast spirit within me. 13 Cast me not away from Thy presence; <u>And take not Thy holy spirit from me.</u>

14 Restore unto me the joy of Thy salvation; And let a willing spirit uphold me.

It was Pentecost when these first believers received the promised Spirit. That day had finally come. Acts

2.1-13:

1 And when the day of Pentecost was fully come, <u>they were all with one accord in one place</u>. 2 And suddenly there came a sound from heaven as of a rushing mighty wind, and it filled all the house where they were sitting. 3 And there appeared unto them cloven tongues like as of fire, and it sat upon each of them. 4 And they were all filled with the Holy [Spirit], and began to speak with other tongues, as the Spirit gave them utterance.

5 <u>And there were dwelling at Jerusalem Jews, devout men, out of every nation under heaven</u>. 6 Now when this was noised abroad, the multitude came together, and were confounded, because that every man heard them speak in his own language.

7 And they were all amazed and marvelled, saying one to another, Behold, are not all these which speak Galilaeans? 8 And how hear we every man in our own tongue, wherein we were born? 9 Parthians, and Medes, and Elamites, and the dwellers in Mesopo-

potamia, and in Judaea, and Cappado-
cia, in Pontus, and Asia, 10 Phrygia, and
Pamphylia, in Egypt, and in the parts
of Libya about Cyrene, and strangers
of Rome, Jews and proselytes, 11 Cretes
and Arabians, we do hear them speak
in our tongues the wonderful works of
G-d.

12 And they were all amazed, and were
in doubt, saying one to another, What
meaneth this? 13 Others mocking said,
These men are full of new wine.

The street were filled with Jews from the surrounding nations. They had come for the festival and now
witnessed these believers, filled with the Spirit, as
they entered into the street.

Peter stood to make a speech to explain what
was happening. Peter, one of the Twelve, stood before the crowd. Verses 14-15:

14 But Peter, standing up with the elev-
en, lifted up his voice, and said unto
them, Ye men of Judaea, and all ye that
dwell at Jerusalem, be this known unto
you, and hearken to my words:

15 For these are not drunken, as ye sup-

pose, seeing it is but the third hour of the day.

He tells them this occurrence was prophesied by the Prophet Joel. Since this concerns the end times, let us look at these verses. Joel 3.1-5:

> 1 And it shall come to pass afterward, That <u>I will pour out My spirit upon all flesh</u>; And your sons and your daughters shall prophesy, Your old men shall dream dreams, Your young men shall see visions; 2 And also upon the servants and upon the handmaids In those days will I pour out My spirit.

> 3 And I will shew wonders in the heavens and in the earth, Blood, and fire, and pillars of smoke. 4 The sun shall be turned into darkness, And the moon into blood, Before the great and terrible day of the LORD come. 5 And it shall come to pass, that whosoever shall call on the name of the LORD shall be delivered; For in mount Zion and in Jerusalem there shall be those that escape, As the LORD hath said, And among the remnant those whom the LORD shall call.

The latter part of this sounds a lot like the words Yeshua spoke in Matthew 24. He answered His disciples' questions about the coming of the end times.

Peter referred to this prophecy as he continued. Acts 2.16-20:

> 16 **But this is that which was spoken by the prophet Joel;**
>
> 17 **And it shall come to pass in the last days, saith G-d, I will pour out my Spirit upon all flesh: and your sons and your daughters shall prophesy, and your young men shall see visions, and your old men shall dream dreams:** 18 **And on my servants and on my handmaidens I will pour out in those days of my Spirit; and they shall prophesy:**
>
> 19 **And I will shew wonders in heaven above, and signs in the earth beneath; blood, and fire, and vapour of smoke:** 20 **The sun shall be turned into darkness, and the moon into blood, before that great and notable day of the Lord come:**

The last seven years will be a time of judgment. Do

you remember when Yeshua read before the synagogue? He stopped mid-verse and went to sit down. Here is the portion He did not read because it was still in the future. "And the day of vengeance of our G-d" (Isa. 61.2). This will be a time of judgment and it is the same time period to which Joel referred.

Although the seven last years will be filled with judgment, there is good news. It is important for the sons and daughters of Abraham to remember this. Peter continues his speech. Verses 21-24:

21 **And it shall come to pass, that whosoever shall call on the name of the Lord shall be saved. 22 Ye men of Israel, hear these words; [Yeshua] of Nazareth, a man approved of G-d among you by miracles and wonders and signs, which G-d did by him in the midst of you, as ye yourselves also know:**

23 **Him, being delivered by the determinate counsel and foreknowledge of G-d, ye have taken, and by wicked hands have crucified and slain: 24 Whom G-d hath raised up, having loosed the pains of death: because it was not possible that he should be**

246

holden of it.

The historic events of the crucifixion, his burial, and the resurrection were just fifty days prior to this festival. Many of those attending were eyewitnesses to these events. Since they were there, no one refuted or denied the facts as stated by Peter.

He continues by speaking about King David. Verses 25-28:

> 25 **For David speaketh concerning him, I foresaw the Lord always before my face, for he is on my right hand, that I should not be moved: 26 Therefore did my heart rejoice, and my tongue was glad; moreover also my flesh shall rest in hope:**
>
> 27 **Because thou wilt not leave my soul in hell, neither wilt thou suffer [allow] thine Holy One to see corruption. 28 Thou hast made known to me the ways of life; thou shalt make me full of joy with thy countenance.**

David believed in the promise of resurrection and had hope of it. G-d loosed the penalty of death because it was not possible that Yeshua HaMashiach could be held by death because He was righteous.

The human body begins to decompose shortly after death. David stated that G-d would not allow His Holy One to see corruption or, in other words, decomposition.

Peter speaks to the men of Israel about David's claim. Verse 29:

> 29 **Men and brethren, let me freely speak unto you of the patriarch David, that he is both dead and buried, and his sepulchre is with us unto this day.**

He speaks of the promise G-d made to David concerning His throne. Verses 30-35:

> 30 **Therefore [David] being a prophet, and knowing that G-d had sworn with an oath to him, that of the fruit of his loins, according to the flesh, he [G-d] would raise up [HaMashiach] to sit on his throne; 31 He seeing this before spake of the resurrection of [HaMashiach], that his soul was not left in hell, neither his flesh did see corruption.**
>
> 32 **This [Yeshua] hath G-d raised up, whereof we all are witnesses. 33 Therefore being by the right hand of G-d exalted, and having received of [from]**

the Father **the promise of the Holy**
[Spirit], **he hath shed forth this, which
ye now see and hear.** 34 For David is
not ascended into the heavens: but he
saith himself, [Psalm 110] The LORD
said unto my Lord, Sit thou on my
right hand, 35 Until I make thy foes thy
footstool.

Peter concludes by making the following public proclamation. Verse 36:

36 Therefore **let all the house of Israel
know** assuredly, that **G-d hath made
that same [Yeshua], whom ye have crucified, both Lord and Christ** [Anoint-
ed].

All the promises G-d made to the fathers are fulfilled in Yeshua Mashiach. In spite of being cut-off
at the end of the sixty-ninth week, the prophecies
will be fulfilled in Him.

Hearing this, they were cut to the quick and
asked Peter what they should do. Peter's response
was not only applicable to the Jews then, but it is also applicable to Jews of today. This is the Gospel of
the Kingdom! Here is Peter's response. Verses 37-
38:

37 Now when they heard this, they were pricked in their heart, and said unto Peter and to the rest of the apostles, <u>Men and brethren, what shall we do?</u>

38 Then Peter said unto them, <u>Repent, and be baptized every one of you in the name of [Yeshua HaMashiach] for the remission of sins, and ye shall receive the gift of the Holy [Spirit].</u>

He instructs those who wish to be saved and enter the Kingdom of Heaven first to repent. The word "repent" means "to stop and turn away from what you are doing." They are to stop sinning, do an about-face, and head back to the ways of G-d according to the Law. Then, they are to be baptized as an outward display of their faith and commitment. The results of these actions will secure for them "the remission of sins." And, at the Coming of the Holy One, their sins will be forgiven.

This Gospel of the Kingdom is intended for the sons and daughters of Abraham. They, like their father Abraham, must "accept by faith" what has been promised to them by G-d. Verses 39-40:

39 For the promise is unto you, and to your children, and to all that are afar

off, even as many as the Lord our G-d shall call. 40 **And with many other words did he testify and exhort, saying, Save yourselves from this untoward generation.**

The promises of the Kingdom Gospel belong to Israel if they will receive them. The true sons and daughters of Israel will believe and hold fast, by faith, to these promises regardless of their present circumstances. Of this they may be confident: the Word of G-d does not change. Israel must believe that what G-d said He will do, He will do. That is faith!

24

Intermission

The word "intermission" means "a cessation of an activity, such as a play or game, only to be resumed afterward." The remainder of the 490 years should have expired long ago. They would have if it were not for this intermission or "temporary suspension" of Daniel's timeline. I call this a "parenthetical interruption."

As we count the seven days towards G-d's restoration, the Fifth Day will end when the last seven years are completed. The suspension will be lifted and the Fifth Day will resume. There are seven years remaining until its completion. What caused the suspension? How long will the suspension last? These are two very good questions that we will now answer.

Following the death, burial, and resurrection of HaMashiach there was a second offer made to

Israel's rulers. Stephen was a devout Jew and believer of Yeshua HaMashiach. He kept the Law and was a righteous man filled with the Spirit. Stephen was falsely charged with blasphemy and brought before the high priest and the rulers. You can read the entire account in Acts 6.9–8.2. Stephen, in his defense, lists Israel's past. It is similar to Yeshua's parable of the landowner and his tenants. Stephen concludes his speech before the rulers of Israel with an indictment. Acts 7.51-53:

> **51 Ye stiffnecked and uncircumcised in heart and ears, ye do always resist the Holy [Spirit]: as your fathers did, so do ye.**

> **52 Which of the prophets have not your fathers persecuted? and they have slain them which shewed before of the coming of the Just One; of whom ye have been now the betrayers and murderers:**

> **53 Who have received the law by the disposition of angels [messengers], and have not kept it.**

With this, the rulers became furious. Verses 54-57:

> **54 When they heard these things, they**

> were cut to the heart, and they gnashed
> on him with their teeth. 55 But he, be-
> ing full of the Holy [Spirit], looked up
> stedfastly into heaven, and saw the
> glory of G-d, and [Yeshua] standing on
> the right hand of G-d,
>
> 56 And said, <u>Behold, I see the heavens
> opened, and the Son of man standing
> on the right hand of G-d</u>. 57 Then they
> cried out with a loud voice, and
> stopped their ears, and ran upon him
> with one accord,

There was something different here. Stephen stated
he saw Yeshua standing on the right hand of G-d
and not sitting on the right hand of G-d. Compare
this to what David wrote in Psalm 110.1:

> 1 The LORD saith unto my lord: '<u>Sit
> thou at My right hand</u>, Until I make
> thine enemies thy footstool.'

Why was Yeshua standing and not sitting? It was a
second offer. Had the rulers of Israel repented,. Yeshua was prepared to return and complete the sev-
en remaining years. However, the rulers rejected it.

They did not believe or repent. Instead, they
had Stephen brought out to be stoned. Acts 7.58-60:

58 And cast him out of the city, and stoned him: and the witnesses laid down their clothes at a young man's feet, whose name was Saul.

59 And they stoned Stephen, calling upon G-d, and saying, Lord [Yeshua] receive my spirit.

60 And he kneeled down, and cried with a loud voice, Lord, lay not this sin to their charge. And when he had said this, he fell asleep.

The crucifixion occurred in 30 CE. Forty years after Israel's rejection of Yeshua HaMashiach, Jerusalem and the temple were destroyed by the Romans in 70 CE. The rulers of Israel had their faith tested. These verses record that failure.

Here, at this point in the biblical narrative, we are introduced to Saul a Pharisee who was taught at the feet of Gamaliel. Verses 8.1-3:

1 And Saul was consenting unto his death. And at that time there was a great persecution against the church which was at Jerusalem; and they were all scattered abroad throughout the regions of Judaea and Samaria, except the apostles.

2 And devout men carried Stephen to his burial, and made great lamentation over him.

3 As for Saul, he made havock of the church, entering into every house, and haling men and women committed them to prison.

Luke, the author of Acts, wrote about the persecution of those who followed the Gospel of the Kingdom – those who by faith were earnestly awaiting the fulfillment of the Davidic Kingdom.

Saul, a zealous Jew, would pursue these new believers and bring them to Jerusalem for punishment. Acts 9.1-2:

1 And Saul, yet [while] breathing out threatenings and slaughter against the disciples of the Lord, went unto the high priest, 2 And desired of him letters to Damascus to the synagogues, that if he found any of this way, whether they were men or women, he might bring them bound unto Jerusalem.

Luke records the confrontation that occurred on the Road to Damascus. It was between Saul and Ha-Mashiach. Verses 3-9:

> 3 And as he journeyed, he came near Damascus: and suddenly there shined round about him a light from heaven: 4 And he fell to the earth, and heard a voice saying unto him, Saul, Saul, why persecutest thou me?

> 5 And he said, Who art thou, Lord? And the Lord said, I am [Yeshua] whom thou persecutest: it is hard for thee to kick against the pricks. 6 And he trembling and astonished said, Lord, what wilt thou have me to do? And the Lord said unto him, Arise, and go into the city, and it shall be told thee what thou must do.

> 7 And the men which journeyed with him stood speechless, hearing a voice, but seeing no man. 8 And Saul arose from the earth; and when his eyes were opened, he saw no man: but they led him by the hand, and brought him into Damascus. 9 And he was three days without sight, and neither did eat nor drink.

We can assume that G-d now had Paul's attention. G-d directed a certain devout follower, Ananias, to go and restore Paul's sight. Ananias was a believer. Verses 10-12:

> 10 **And there was a certain disciple at Damascus, named Ananias; and to him said the Lord in a vision, Ananias. And he said, Behold, I am here, Lord.**

> 11 **And the Lord said unto him, Arise, and go into the street which is called Straight, and enquire in the house of Judas for one called Saul, of Tarsus: for, behold, he prayeth,** 12 **And hath seen in a vision a man named Ananias coming in, and putting his hand on him, that he might receive his sight.**

Paul's reputation had preceded him and Ananias was both afraid and hesitant. Notice G-d's response to Ananias. Verses 13-16:

> 13 **Then Ananias answered, Lord, I have heard by many of this man, how much evil he hath done to thy saints at Jerusalem:** 14 **And here he hath authority from the chief priests to bind all that call on thy name.**

15 But the Lord said unto him, <u>Go thy way: for he is a chosen vessel unto me, to bear my name before the Gentiles, and kings, and the children of Israel:</u> **16** For I will shew him how great things he must suffer for my name's sake.

G-d told Ananias what He would use Paul for His purpose. Paul would be His chosen vessel to carry a message to the Gentiles. This might be unbelievable if G-d had not provided the example of Jonah. G-d said to Moses, "I will be gracious to whom I will be gracious, and will show mercy on whom I will show mercy" (Exodus 33.19). Paul's sight was restored and he ate some food. Look at the change. Verse 20-22:

20 And straightway [immediately] he preached Christ [the Anointed] in the synagogues, that he is the Son of G-d. **21** But all that heard him were amazed, and said; Is not this he that destroyed them which called on this name in Jerusalem, and came hither for that intent, that he might bring them bound unto the chief priests?

22 But Saul increased the more in strength, and confounded the Jews which dwelt at Damascus, proving that

this is very Christ [the Anointed].

This event marks the beginning of the intermission. Paul wrote thirteen books: Romans to Philemon. They were written to the Gentiles. The great city of Nineveh was offered repentance by Jonah. Now, the Gentiles will be offered repentance by the Apostle Paul.

When we began this book, I promised that I would not preach to the Jews any gospel message other than their own. I stand by that promise. Therefore, to understand this parenthetical interruption of Daniel's timeline, I recommend you read *Letters To Theophilus*. It goes into great detail concerning the separate Gospel of Grace. It is important that you see clearly there are two distinct gospels. One was preached by Yeshua HaMashiach and the Twelve during His earthly ministry. It was intended for the lost sheep of the house of Israel. (See Matt. 10.6; 15.24.) The other gospel was preached by Paul to the Gentiles.

There was a meeting between these two groups. Apostles Peter and Paul only met a few times in the course of their ministries. Here is a record of their meeting in Jerusalem. Galatians 2.6-9:

6 But of these who seemed to be somewhat, (whatsoever they were, it maketh

no matter to me: G-d accepteth no man's person:) for they who seemed to be somewhat in conference added nothing to me:

7 But contrariwise, when <u>they saw that the gospel of the uncircumcision was committed unto me, as the gospel of the circumcision was unto Peter;</u> 8 (For he that wrought effectually in Peter to the apostleship of the circumcision, the same was mighty in me toward the Gentiles:)

9 And when James, Cephas [Peter], and John, who seemed to be pillars, perceived the grace that was given unto me, they gave to me and Barnabas the right hands of fellowship; <u>that we should go unto the heathen, and they unto the circumcision.</u>

When did the suspension of the timeline begin? Acts is the fifth book in the New Covenant. The following is found in the last chapter. Acts 28.16-22:

16 And when we came to Rome, the centurion delivered the prisoners to the captain of the guard: but Paul was

suffered [allowed] to dwell by himself with a soldier that kept him.

17 And it came to pass, that after three days Paul called the chief of the Jews [in Rome] together: and when they were come together, he said unto them, Men and brethren, though I have committed nothing against the people, or customs of our fathers, yet was I delivered prisoner from Jerusalem into the hands of the Romans. 18 Who, when they had examined me, would have let me go, because there was no cause of death in me.

19 But when the Jews spake against it, I was constrained to appeal unto Caesar; not that I had ought [anything] to accuse my nation of. 20 For this cause therefore have I called for you, to see you, and to speak with you: because that for the hope of Israel I am bound with this chain.

21 And they said unto him, We neither received letters out of Judaea concerning thee, neither any of the brethren that came shewed or spake any harm of thee. 22 But we desire to hear of thee

what thou thinkest: for as concerning this sect, we know that every where it is spoken against.

They arranged with the guards to come back to meet with Paul and hear what he had to say. Verses 23-24:

23 And when they had appointed him a day, there came many to him into his lodging; to whom he expounded and testified the kingdom of G-d, persuading them concerning [Yeshua], both out of the law of Moses, and out of the prophets, from morning till evening. 24 And some believed the things which were spoken, and some believed not.

Up to this point in time, nothing had changed: some believed and some did not. Verses 25-27:

25 And when they agreed not among themselves, they departed, after that Paul had spoken one word, Well spake the Holy [Spirit] by Esaias [Isaiah] the prophet unto our fathers,

26 Saying, <u>Go unto this people, and say, Hearing ye shall hear, and shall not understand; and seeing ye shall see,</u>

and not perceive:

27 For the heart of this people is waxed [grown] gross, and their ears are dull of hearing, and their eyes have they closed; lest they should see with their eyes, and hear with their ears, and understand with their heart, and should be converted, and I should heal them.

Paul quoted Isaiah (vv. 6.9-10) to these Jews. So, what suspended the timeline until the end times and the establishment of the Kingdom? Consider the following proclamation. Acts 28.28-29:

28 Be it known therefore unto you, that the salvation of G-d is sent unto the Gentiles, and that they will hear it.

29 And when he had said these words, the Jews departed, and had great reasoning among themselves.

G-d chose to temporarily offer salvation to the Gentiles. Why? Like the those in Nineveh, they will hear it.

Since Abraham, there has always been two distinct groups: Jews and non-Jews. G-d chose Israel from out of all the other nations. In Paul's ministry, however, something happens. A third group is created. Paul described this third group as being "neither Jew nor Greek" (Gal. 3.28). As this subject is not part of this book, we will not go further. For more details concerning G-d's ministry to the Gentiles, consider reading *Letters To Theophilus – Are You Ready For The End Times?* We have identified when this suspension began. Now, we have another question: "When will Daniel's timeline resume?"

The timeline will resume at the occurrence of a certain event. The word "rapture" means "catching away." This third group of people who are "neither Jew nor Gentile" will be removed. It is upon their removal that the seven remaining years of Daniel's prophecy will resume. We must remain focused on the glorious destiny of Israel. The parenthetical interruption or temporary suspension began with the Apostle Paul. It continues through what is called the "Time of the Gentiles" currently working towards its conclusion. Concerning the Jews, the suspension will end when this new group, created by G-d, is removed. This will leave the two original groups, Israel and the Gentiles, for the final event known as the "end times."

25

Israel's Eternal High Priest

The fifth book in the New Covenant is the Acts of the Apostles. Here, we find the beginning of the "temporary suspension" of Daniel's timeline. Salvation is sent to the Gentiles as G-d knows "that they will hear it." Acts 28.28:

> 28 **Be it known therefore unto you, that the salvation of G-d is sent unto the Gentiles, and that they will hear it.**

Nothing has changed for the Jews. G-d's plans and promises to them are still in effect. However, the timeline is currently in abeyance. Daniel's other prophecy concerning the Time of the Gentiles runs concurrent with his prophecy concerning Israel. His relationship with Israel cannot be compared to any other as there is none like it. Both timelines will converge in the end.

Like the Torah, the first five books of the New Covenant (New Testament) were written to the Jews. The last of the five, Acts, is a transitional book as it explains the temporary suspension. Please indulge me for a moment as I introduce a "key" to understanding the books of the New Covenant. Find a large paperclip. In the New Covenant, find the books beginning with Romans and ending with Philemon and place them between your fingers. Slide the large paperclip of them to separate them from the beginning and ending of the New Covenant. Now, allow me to explain.

With the Pauline epistles held firmly in the middle, there are two sides. The first group before, we have already reviewed. They record the arrival, ministry, and message proclaimed to Israel by Ha-Mashiach. The Apostle John summaries the result in John 1:10-11:

> 10 **He was in the world, and the world was made by him, and the world knew him not. 11 He came unto his own, and his own received him not.**

The books that follow the Pauline epistles begin with Hebrews and end with Revelation. These latter letters were also written to Israel for a very important reason. G-d knew that Israel would need support and encouragement to be faithful and

268

endure unto the end. Therefore, the second group deals with the actual occurrence of "Jacob's Time of Trouble." So, if we skip over the Paul's letters, then the first book we come to is Hebrews.

Look at the opening words. Is there any question this letter was written to the Jews? Hebrews 1.1-5:

> 1 G-d, who at sundry [different] times and in divers manners [different ways] spake in time past <u>unto the fathers</u> by the prophets, 2 [Who] <u>Hath in these last days spoken unto us by his Son</u> [Yeshua HaMashiach], whom he [G-d] hath appointed heir of all things, by [through] whom also he [G-d] made the worlds;

> 3 Who [Yeshua] being the brightness of his [G-d's] glory, and the express image of his [G-d's] person, and upholding all things by the word of his power, when he had by himself purged our [Israel's] sins, [Yeshua] sat down on the right hand of the Majesty on high [Psalm 110];

> 4 Being made so much better than the angels, as he [Yeshua] hath by inher-

itance obtained a more excellent name than they. 5 For unto which of the angels said he [G-d] at any time, Thou art my Son, this day have I begotten thee? [Psalm 1:7] And again, I will be to him a Father, and he shall be to me a Son?

The following verses refer specifically to the coming Eternal King who is the heir to David's throne. (*cf.* 2 Sam. 7.13-14.) Notice that His inheritance includes the nations, or Gentiles, who remain at the end of the seven years. Psalm 1.6:-8:

6 'Truly it is I that have established My king Upon Zion, My holy mountain.'

7 I will tell of the decree: <u>The LORD said unto me: 'Thou art My son, This day have I begotten thee.</u>

8 <u>Ask of Me, and I will give the nations for thine inheritance, And the ends of the earth for thy possession.</u>

Now, let us look at the words spoken by G-d to the Prophet Nathan concerning this same heir to the throne of David. 1 Chronicles 17.13-14:

13 I will be to him for a father, and he shall be to Me for a son; and I will not

take My mercy away from him, as I took it from him that was before thee;

14 but <u>I will settle him in My house and in My kingdom for ever; and his throne shall be established for ever.</u>'

We know that there is only one G-d; there is no other. Each morning and evening these words are spoken. Deuteronomy 6.4:

4 HEAR, O ISRAEL: THE LORD OUR G-D, THE LORD IS ONE. 5 And thou shalt love the LORD thy G-d with all thy heart, and with all thy soul, and with all thy might.

Most would say that this means there is one singular G-d. Contrary to what many people believe, making Yeshua HaMashiach equal with G-d does not go against monotheism. We are going to look at a few examples to see if we can confirm the truth of Shema Yisrael.

Consider the union between a husband and his wife. Are they not said to be one? According to G-d, they are. Genesis 1.24:

24 Therefore shall a man leave his father and his mother, and shall cleave

unto his wife, and <u>they shall be one flesh</u>.

Here are two individuals, yet G-d sees them as one. At a synagogue, there is a minyan and, of these men, how many of them would say they are the son of their father? How many would say they are the husband of their wife? And, how many would say they are the father of their children? Yet, they are not three, but one. Although, this might apply to their office or role and not their person. Let us consider water, ice, and steam. These are three different physical states of one compound comprised of two parts hydrogen and one part oxygen. In spite of their different states, they are still water.

As human, we all have limited abilities. We can only define G-d as He defines Himself in His Word. Anything that goes beyond that is hyperbole. Therefore, the understanding of G-d as the union of G-d, Son, and Spirit can only be understood by the inspired word of G-d. We can say "The LORD our G-d in One" and know that it is true because G-d Himself has said it in His word. Anything that G-d adds as an explanation of Himself cannot negate what He has already stated. We can only understand G-d through His revelation to us.

Referring to Israel as sheep, Yeshua said, "My Father, which gave them me, is greater than all; and no man is able to pluck them out of my Father's hand. I and my Father are one" (Jn. 10:29-30). Philip, a disciple, asked Yeshua to show them the Father. To which, He responded, "Have I been so long time with you, and yet hast thou not known me, Philip? . . . he that hath seen me hath seen the Father . . . Believe me that I am in the Father, and the Father in me" (Jn, 14:9-11).

Let us consider this. The position of Ha-Mashiach has three offices. These are: Prophet, Priest, and King. Yet, He is One. Allow me to explain. In the four gospels, Yeshua stated that He does not speak His Own words, but only the words given to Him by His Father. That means His role during His earthly ministry was that of Prophet. Also, we know from prophecy that HaMashiach will be the eternal King Who sits upon David's throne. He will return as King to defend His people Israel. He will defeat their enemies. What about the second office of Priest?

As Israel continues to wait for His return as King, there remains the office of Priest. When the Mosaic Law was first instituted, it also created the Levitical Priesthood. This was for good reason. G-d knew that all men sin. All men fall short of G-d's glory or perfection. Sin had to be dealt with. G-d created the priesthood. They were tasked with the responsibility of interceding between sinful Israel and their perfect G-d. So, the last office of Ha-Mashiach is the office of High Priest.

Now, let us return to the book of Hebrews. Again, this book was written specifically to Israel and not written to Christians as many contend. For a detailed explanation, see my commentary entitled *Hebrews: Dispensationally Considered*. Hebrews 2.14-16:

> 14 **Forasmuch then as the children are partakers of flesh and blood, he [Yeshua] also himself likewise took part of the same [by being born of a woman]; that through death he [Yeshua] might destroy him [Satan] that had the power of death, that is, the devil;**

> 15 **And deliver them [Israel] who through fear of death were all their lifetime subject to bondage. 16 For verily he [Yeshua] took not on him [Himself] the nature of angels; but he [Yeshua] took on him <u>the seed of Abraham</u>.**

Since Israel could not save itself, G-d Himself must save Israel. How can this be done? Sin is the power of death under which all men are in bondage. Here is G-d's solution. The LORD Himself would provide a Sacrifice! This is much like the story of Abraham who was willing to sacrifice his only son, yet G-d Himself provided a sacrifice. Genesis 22:10-13:

> 10 **And Abraham stretched forth his hand, and took the knife to slay his son.** 11 **And the angel of the LORD called unto him out of heaven, and said, Abraham, Abraham: and he said, Here am I.** 12 **And he said, Lay not thine hand upon the lad, neither do thou any thing unto him: for now I know that thou fearest G-d, seeing thou hast not withheld thy son, thine only son from me.**
>
> 13 **And Abraham lifted up his eyes, and looked, and behold behind him a ram caught in a thicket by his horns: and Abraham went and took the ram, and offered him up for a burnt offering in the stead of his son.**

Abraham believed G-d and would not spare his own son. For this reason, G-d Himself will do for the children of Abraham what their father would have done for G-d.

The sacrificial Lamb must be perfect – without

spot or blemish. Yeshua HaMashiach, having fulfilled all the requirements of the Law, was perfect before G-d. This Lamb, having paid the penalty for sin, is now able to represent His brethren before the Holy G-d. Hebrews 2:17-18:

> 17 **Wherefore in all things it behoved [was right, necessary or useful for] him to be made like unto his brethren [the children of Abraham], that he [Yeshua] might be a merciful and faithful high priest in things pertaining to G-d, to make reconciliation for the sins of the people.**

> 18 **For in that he himself [Yeshua Ha-Mashiach] hath suffered being tempted, he is able to succour [to give relief to] them that are tempted.**

It is clear that the writer of Hebrews is addressing the people of Israel. Hebrews 3.1-6:

> 1 **Wherefore, [Israel] holy brethren, partakers of the heavenly calling, consider the Apostle [Messenger] and High Priest of our profession, [HaMashiach Yeshua];**

> 2 **Who was faithful to him [G-d] that**

276

appointed him, as also Moses was faithful in all his house.

3 For this man [Yeshua] was counted worthy of more glory than Moses, inasmuch as he who hath builded the house hath more honour than the house. 4 For every house is builded by some man; but he that built all things is G-d.

5 And Moses verily was faithful in all his house, as a servant, for a testimony of those things which were to be spoken after; 6 But [HaMashiach] as a son over his own house; whose house are we [Israel], if we <u>hold fast the confidence and the rejoicing of the hope firm unto the end</u>.

This is consistent with the words spoken by Yeshua to His Twelve concerning the end times. Matthew 24.13:

13 But he that shall endure unto the end, the same shall be saved.

The requirements of the Mosaic Law still continue. HaMashiach came not to abolish the Law, but to fulfill it. As the High Priest, He is greater than any prior priest of Aaron because He will never die. Like their King, He will serve as the High Priest of true and faithful Israel forever! Who is true and faithful Israel?

True and faithful Israel are those who receive and believe the Word of G-d. They demonstrate their faith by their love and the actions. Having their faith based upon the Word of G-d, they can continue with a hope that will "endure unto the end."

26

Faith Hall of Fame

True Israel are those individuals who receive and believe the Word of G-d written in His book. Israel must keep that faith and endure unto the end. Here is a chapter you will find encouraging. Hebrews 11 is referred to as the "Faith Hall of Fame." All those mentioned are sons and daughters of their father Abraham. I say that because you will find Abraham referred to as "the father of faith." This will support the idea that true Israel are those who, like their father Abraham, have faith.

We start by defining the word "faith." Hebrews 11.1-2:

> 1 Now <u>faith is the substance of things hoped for, the evidence of things not seen</u>. 2 For by it the elders obtained a good report.

The words "good report" mean that G-d recognized their faith because they believed His Word. Verse 3:

> 3 **Through faith we understand that the worlds were framed by the word of G-d, so that things which are seen were not made of things which do appear.**

Before G-d spoke, there was nothing. He spoke Creation into its existence. Faithful Jews celebrate this event every Shabbat. Here is a list of people who showed their faith through their actions. Verses 3-5:

> 4 **By faith Abel offered unto G-d a more excellent sacrifice than Cain, by which he obtained witness that he was righteous, G-d testifying of his gifts: and by it he being dead yet speaketh.**
>
> 5 **By faith Enoch was translated that he should not see death; and was not found, because G-d had translated him: for before his translation he had this testimony, that he pleased G-d.**

The author pauses the list for a moment to make an important point. It is a person's "faith" that pleases G-d. Verses 6:

> 6 **But without faith it is impossible to**

please him: for he that cometh to G-d must believe that he is, and that he [G-d] is a rewarder of them that diligently seek him.

Having made this point, the list of people continues. Verses 7-12:

7 **By faith** Noah, being warned of G-d of things not seen as yet, moved with fear, prepared an ark to the saving of his house; by the which he condemned the world, and became heir of the righteousness which is by faith.

8 **By faith** Abraham, when he was called to go out into a place which he should after receive for an inheritance, obeyed; and he went out, not knowing whither he went. 9 **By faith** he sojourned in the land of promise, as in a strange country, dwelling in tabernacles with Isaac and Jacob, the heirs with him of the same promise: 10 For he looked for a city which hath foundations, whose builder and maker is G-d.

11 **Through faith** also Sara herself received strength to conceive seed, and was delivered of a child when she was

past age, because <u>she judged him faith-ful who had promised</u>. 12 **Therefore sprang there even of one, and him as good as dead, so many as the stars of the sky in multitude, and as the sand which is by the sea shore innumerable.**

Both Sarah and Abraham were great in age and their ability to produce children naturally was "as good as dead." Yet, they believed G-d's promise for a son and He blessed them with Isaac. The children of Israel are here today because of Abraham's faith.

The list is paused. Some comments are made concerning these representatives of faith who had not received the promises, but still had faith. Verses 13-16:

> 13 **<u>These all died in faith</u>, <u>not having received the promises, but having seen them afar off</u>, and were persuaded of them, and embraced them, and confessed that they were strangers and pilgrims on the earth.** 14 **For they that say such things declare plainly that they seek a country.**
>
> 15 **And truly, if they had been mindful of that country from whence they came**

out, they might have had opportunity to have returned. 16 But now they desire a better country, that is, an heavenly: wherefore G-d is not ashamed to be called their G-d: for he hath prepared for them a city.

They continue to seek this "better country" by faith while they wait and long for the promises with hope. That hope is based upon believing in the promises made to Israel and the One Who gave them. Remember this. For faith is "the substance of things hoped for" and "the evidence of things not seen" (v.11.1).

As it continues, the focus turned to Abraham. Verses 17-19:

17 By faith Abraham, when he was tried, offered up Isaac: and he that had received the promises offered up his only begotten son, 18 Of whom it was said, That in Isaac shall thy seed be called: 19 Accounting that G-d was able to raise him up, even from the dead; from whence also he received him in a figure.

The legacy of the children of Abraham is faith! Verses 20-22:

20 **By faith** Isaac blessed Jacob and Esau concerning things to come. 21 By faith Jacob, when he was a dying, blessed both the sons of Joseph; and worshipped, leaning upon the top of his staff.

22 **By faith** Joseph, when he died, made mention of the departing of the children of Israel; and gave commandment concerning his bones.

We come to Moses and his faith. Verses 23-28:

23 **By faith** Moses, when he was born, was hid three months of his parents, because they saw he was a proper child; and they were not afraid of the king's commandment.

24 **By faith** Moses, when he was come to years, refused to be called the son of Pharaoh's daughter; 25 Choosing rather to suffer affliction with the people of G-d, than to enjoy the pleasures of sin for a season; 26 Esteeming the reproach of [HaMashiach] greater riches than the treasures in Egypt: for he had respect unto the recompence of the reward.

27 **By faith** he forsook Egypt, not fearing the wrath of the king: for he endured, as seeing him who is invisible.

28 **Through faith** he kept the passover, and the sprinkling of blood, lest he that destroyed the firstborn should touch them.

All these individuals deserved honorable mention because they actions demonstrated their faith. They believed G-d's word. What about the people of Israel? They too exhibited faith. Verses 29-30:

29 **By faith** they passed through the Red sea as by dry land: which the Egyptians assaying to do were drowned.

30 **By faith** the walls of Jericho fell down, after they were compassed about seven days.

In the next verse, consider its poignancy. We find a prostitute included. Faith covers a multitude of sin. Her life was spared because she believed when the rest of Jericho perished. Verse 31:

31 **By faith** the harlot Rahab perished not with them that believed not, when she had received the spies with peace.

From this, we see that "faith" is not based upon the perfection of an individual. It is based upon their choice to believe G-d's Word.

The author stated the list could go on and on since there are many within Abraham's lineage who exhibited their " faith." Verses 32-38:

> 32 And what shall I more say? for the time would fail me to tell of Gedeon, and of Barak, and of Samson, and of Jephthae; of David also, and Samuel, and of the prophets: 33 Who through faith subdued kingdoms, wrought righteousness, obtained promises, stopped the mouths of lions,

> 34 Quenched the violence of fire, escaped the edge of the sword, out of weakness were made strong, waxed valiant in fight, turned to fight the armies of the aliens. 35 Women received their dead raised to life again: and others were tortured, not accepting deliverance; that they might obtain a better resurrection:

> 36 And others had trial of cruel mock-

ings and scourgings, yea, moreover of bonds and imprisonment: 37 They were stoned, they were sawn asunder, were tempted, were slain with the sword: they wandered about in sheepskins and goatskins; being destitute, afflicted, tormented;

38 (Of whom the world was not worthy:) they wandered in deserts, and in mountains, and in dens and caves of the earth.

All of those mentioned had one thing in common. Each acted upon their faith by believing G-d's Word. Their actions were testimonies of that faith. The chapter closes with an important point. Verses 39-40:

39 And these all, having obtained a good report through faith, received not the promise: 40 G-d having provided some better thing for us, that they without us should not be made perfect.

The words "having obtained a good report" mean their actions were based upon their faith and, therefore, acceptable to G-d. They were approved through their testimonies. They acted on their faith and by their actions, they proved their faith. Even though they had not yet received the promises, they waited and continue to unwaveringly believe G-d. They endured by patiently and faithfully waited for the fulfillment of the promises.

27

Seven Last Years

The purpose of this book is to focus on the glorious destiny of Israel. At this point, those who followed Paul's Gospel of Grace have been removed. This event, called "the Rapture," marks the beginning of the last seven years. Now, Gentiles have no hope other than to bless Israel during the Tribulation. How G-d deals with the Nations depends on whether they bless or curse Israel. We find this in G-d's promise to Abraham. Genesis 12.3:

> 3 And <u>I will bless them that bless thee,</u> and <u>him that curseth thee will I curse;</u> and in thee shall all the families of the earth be blessed.

In the end, their blessings will continue through Abraham whose children are a royal a priesthood who serve G-d and intercede on their behalf. Two groups remain: Israel and the Nations.

Next, we will look at the book of Revelation. This is the last book in the Bible and it concludes the New Covenant. The Apostle John, one of the Twelve, was the last apostle living. He recorded what will happen in the future as G-d concludes the restoration of His Creation. We will see the judgments upon G-d's enemies and the unfaithful who rejected His Word. We will see the glorious destiny of Israel and the shining New Jerusalem. Since Revelation prophetic, symbols are often used. This style of writing is "allegorical" and not literal. The word "allegory" means "a representation of abstract ideas or principles by use of characters, figures, or events in a dramatic or pictorial narrative."

The word "revelation" means "the revealing of something that is hidden." Revelation has two primary purposes. (1) G-d is revealing the consummation of His plan to restore His Creation. (2) G-d is revealing His Son. He is the eternal King Who will reign over Creation from Jerusalem . . . forever. There is much detail in this book. For our purpose, we will only focus on the highlights. The timeline remains our focus. Here are two facts you should know before we begin. First, the seven years are broken down into two equal parts. These are referred to as: three and one-half years, forty-two months, or 1260 days. Second, the first half is bad while the second half is really-really bad. This latter period is called "the Great Tribulation."

These are its opening verses from Revelation 1.1-3:

1 **The Revelation of [Yeshua HaMashi-ach], which G-d gave unto him [Ye-shua] , to shew unto his servants things which must shortly come to pass; and he sent and signified it by his angel unto his servant John: 2 Who bare rec-ord of the word of G-d, and of the tes-timony of [Yeshua HaMashiach], and of all things that he saw.**

3 **Blessed is he that readeth, and they that hear the words of this prophecy, and keep those things which are writ-ten therein: for the time is at hand.**

Those who read, understand, and believe these words of prophecy will be blessed. How so? They will be blessed with understanding the workings of G-d. When others around them are in utter chaos and panic, they will have faith in G-d's Word know-ing all that He said will shortly come to pass.

As one of the Twelve, John taught the Gospel of the Kingdom. It is the same gospel message taught by HaMashiach. John wrote to encourage and educate the Kingdom Believers while he was in exile on the Isle of Patmos. Verses 9-11:

9 I John, who also am your brother, and companion in tribulation, and in the kingdom and patience of [Yeshua Ha-Mashiach], was in the isle that is called Patmos, for the word of G-d, and for the testimony of [Yeshua HaMashiach].

10 I was in the Spirit on the Lord's day, and heard behind me a great voice, as of a trumpet, **11** Saying, I am Alpha and Omega, the first and the last: and, What thou seest, write in a book, . . .

This revelation was given to the Apostle John by Yeshua HaMashiach. John watches the future play out as G-d's promises and prophecies to Israel are fulfilled. Verse 19:

19 Write the things which thou hast seen, and the things which are, and the things which shall be hereafter;

Israel's faith must be accompanied by works. For them, their works or actions are the evidence of their faith. James is another of Twelve who wrote to the Kingdom Believers. James wrote a verse that many Christians falsely use to support their replacement theology. However, we will see this applies to Israel alone. James 2.18-24:

18 Yea, a man may say, Thou hast faith, and I have works: shew me thy faith without thy works, and <u>I will shew thee my faith by my works</u>. **19** Thou believest that there is one G-d; thou doest well: the devils also believe, and tremble. **20** But wilt thou know, O vain man, that <u>faith without works is dead?</u>

21 Was not <u>Abraham our father justified by works</u>, when he had offered Isaac his son upon the altar? **22** Seest thou how faith wrought [made] with his works, and by works was faith made perfect?

23 And the scripture was fulfilled which saith, Abraham believed G-d, and it was imputed unto him for righteousness: and he was called the Friend of G-d. **24** Ye see then how that by works a man is justified, and not by faith only.

Hold up for a moment. I would like to address any Christians reading this book. How can we know that James wrote this letter to the Jews? First, Paul is the Apostle to the Gentiles. Second, go to the beginning of James' letter and read his greeting. James 1.1:

1 James, a servant of G-d and of the [Yeshua HaMashiach], <u>to the twelve tribes which are scattered abroad,</u> greetings.

With tongue in cheek, I ask the Christians, "Which tribe of Israel are you from?"

All of the letters, after Paul's letters, were written to the Jews. For this reason, many refer to them as "the Hebrew epistles." They provide instruction and encouragement for the Jews during the coming tribulation. They must believe G-d's Word and show this faith by their actions. How are Kingdom Believers to do this? Matthew 22.36-40:

36 Master, which is the great commandment in the law?

37 [Yeshua] said unto him, Thou shalt love the Lord thy G-d with all thy heart, and with all thy soul, and with all thy mind. 38 This is the first and great commandment.

39 And the second is like unto it, Thou shalt love thy neighbour as thyself. 40 On these two commandments hang all the law and the prophets.

In Matthew 24, Yeshua spoke about the end times and the need for believers to "endure unto the end." The Gospel of the Kingdom is the good news of the coming Kingdom. Its message will be preached unto "all nations" during these seven years. Verse 24.13-14:

> 13 **But he that shall endure unto the end, the same shall be saved.** 14 **And this gospel of the kingdom shall be preached in all the world for a witness unto all nations; and then shall the end come.**

James wrote "to the twelve tribes which are scattered abroad" among the nations. James 5.8-11:

> 8 **Be ye also patient; stablish your hearts: for the coming of the Lord draweth nigh.**
>
> 9 **Grudge not one against another, brethren, lest ye be condemned: behold, the judge standeth before the door.** 10 **Take, my brethren, the prophets, who have spoken in the name of the Lord, for [as] an example of suffering affliction, and of patience.**
>
> 11 **Behold, we count them happy which**

endure. Ye have heard of the patience of Job, and have seen the end of the Lord; that the Lord is very pitiful [One Who takes pity], and of tender mercy.

Like Job, Israel must continue steadfast in their faith and endure unto the end and they will receive their reward.

We will consider the words of two prophets concerning the seven-year period. First, we have the Prophet Joel 2.1-3:

1 **Blow ye the horn in Zion, And sound an alarm in My holy mountain; Let all the inhabitants of the land tremble; For the day of the LORD cometh, For it is at hand;**

2 **A day of darkness and gloominess, A day of clouds and thick darkness, As blackness spread upon the mountains; A great people and a mighty, There hath not been ever the like, Neither shall be any more after them, Even to the years of many generations.**

3 **A fire devoureth before them, And behind them a flame blazeth; The land is as the garden of Eden before them,**

And behind them a desolate wilderness; Yea, and nothing escapeth them

Second, we will close with the Prophet, Jeremiah who warned about trouble and judgment coming. It will be a great testing, but for those who endure, there is a promise. There is hope. Jeremiah 30.23-31.1:

> 23 Behold, a storm of the LORD is gone forth in fury, A sweeping storm; it shall whirl upon the head of the wicked. 24 The fierce anger of the LORD shall not return, Until He have executed, and till He have performed The purposes of His heart; In the end of days ye shall consider it.

> 1 At that time, saith the LORD, Will I be the G-d of all the families of Israel, And they shall be My people.

The next chapter will be a continuation and conclusion of the seven years as G-d moves to establish the Kingdom and the reign of its Eternal King.

28

The Thousand Years

We did not go into a details of the judgments made during the Tribulation. Daniel's 490 years are complete. Now, we will focus on the fulfillment of Israel's promises and prophecies. Daniel had another prophecy concerning the Gentiles that ran concurrent with the 490 years. It has also been completed. The dominance of the Gentile Nations has come to its end. Here is a list of the promises that G-d told Daniel He would fulfill:

(1) finish the transgression, and make an end of sin,
(2) forgive iniquity, and bring in everlasting righteousness,
(3) seal up vision and prophecy, and
(4) anoint the most holy.

So, let us see how G-d fulfills Israel's promises and prophecies.

The New Covenant was foretold by Jeremiah and revealed by Yeshua HaMashiach at His last Passover Seder. We are at the point where it will be put into effect. Jeremiah 31.31-34:

> 31 Behold, <u>the days come</u>, saith the LORD, <u>that I will make a new covenant with the house of Israel, and with the house of Judah;</u> 32 not according to the covenant that I made with their fathers in the day that I took them by the hand to bring them out of the land of Egypt; forasmuch as they broke My covenant, although I was a lord over them, saith the LORD.

> 33 But this is the covenant that I will make with the house of Israel after those days, saith the LORD, <u>I will put My law in their inward parts, and in their heart will I write it; and I will be their G-d, and they shall be My people;</u>

> 34 and they shall teach no more every man his neighbour, and every man his brother, saying: 'Know the LORD'; for they shall all know Me, from the least of them unto the greatest of them, saith the LORD; <u>for I will forgive their iniquity, and their sin will I remember no</u>

more.

Israel had patiently waited for all this to be fulfilled. Now, that time has come. As we move to the finale of the book of Revelation, one can only stand in awe as G-d consummates His promises to Israel.

The Sixth Day

The Sixth Day is another period of time called "the Millennial Age." It immediately follows the Tribulation. It comprises one thousand years and is the period of restoration. This length of time is mentioned twice in the following verses. Revelation 20.1-3:

> 1 **And I saw an angel come down from heaven, having the key of the bottomless pit and a great chain in his hand.** 2 **And he laid hold on the dragon, that old serpent, which is the Devil, and [also called] Satan, and bound him a thousand years,** 3 **And cast him into the bottomless pit, and shut him up, and set a seal upon him, that he should deceive the nations no more, till [until] the thousand years should be fulfilled: and after that he must be loosed [released for] a little season.**

Yeshua spoke about those who will endure. They are the ones who keep their faith for the seven years of tribulation. This Sixth Day is final preparation for the coming Eternal Shabbat – the Seventh Day.

During these one thousand years, there will be a "dispensing" of judgment. Satan will be the first to be judged for what he has done. He will be imprisoned for this period of restoration. This would be a temporary incarceration and prevent him from deceiving the nations. In addition to judgment, there will be a period of purification for those who endured. Some of the nations survived and they will be blessed if they blessed the children of Abraham. The Law which is still in effect will be written upon the hearts of G-d's people.

Those who were faithful to Yeshua HaMashiach and beheaded during the Tribulation will be rewarded. Verse 4:

> 4 And I saw thrones, and they sat upon them, and judgment was given unto them: and I saw the souls of them that were beheaded for the witness of [Yeshua], and for the word of G-d, and which had not worshipped the beast, neither his image, neither had received his mark upon their foreheads, or in their hands; and they lived and reigned

with [HaMashiach] a thousand years.

They preached the Gospel of the Kingdom during the tribulation and were put to death because of their testimony. There were 144,000 witnesses who will be rewarded by reigning with HaMashiach for one thousand years. These will be the first who are resurrected because of their faith and allegiance to HaMashiach. This will be the "first resurrection" from the dead. Verses 5-6:

> 5 **But the rest of the dead lived not again until the thousand years were finished. This is the first resurrection.**
>
> 6 **Blessed and holy is he that hath part in the first resurrection: on such the second death hath no power, but they shall be priests of G-d and of [Ha-Mashiach], and shall reign with him a thousand years.**

At the end of the one thousand years, Satan will be loosed for a short time. It will not be long until he proves he has not changed. In spite of the one-thousand-year incarceration, Satan will be undeterred. He gathers many from the nations together to make war against G-d and His people. The size of their army is described as "the number of whom is as the sand of the sea." Their moment of defiance against G-d is short lived ending with a sudden and violent judgment from G-d. Verses 7-9:

> 7 **And when the thousand years are expired, Satan shall be loosed out of his prison, 8 And shall go out to deceive the nations which are in the four quarters of the earth, Gog and Magog, to gather them together to battle: the number of whom is as the sand of the sea.**

> 9 **And they went up on the breadth of the earth, and compassed the camp of the saints [G-d's people] about, and the beloved city [Jerusalem]: and fire came down from G-d out of heaven, and devoured them.**

Satan has been the father of lies since the beginning. He will deceive the Nations one last time and his punishment will be for eternity. Verse 10:

> 10 **And the devil that deceived them was cast into the lake of fire and brimstone, where the beast and the false prophet are, and shall be tormented day and night for ever and ever.**

The following judgment is referred to as "the Great

White Throne Judgment." This singular event is the final judgment. It leads to the Second Death which is described later. John saw the details of this event as an eyewitness in his vision. The scene he describes is befitting for such a serious occasion. The earth and heaven flee from the face of Him Who is about to pronounce this dreaded but necessary judgment. All the dead, from all the ages past, will be summoned to rise again for their arraignment. As they stand before HaMashiach, the book of deeds and the book of life will be opened. Verses 11-13:

11 And I saw a great white throne, and him that sat on it, from whose face the earth and the heaven fled away; and there was found no place for them.

12 And I saw the dead, small and great, stand before G-d; and the books were opened: and another book was opened, which is the book of life: and the dead were judged out of those things which were written in the books, according to their works.

13 And the sea gave up the dead which were in it; and death and hell delivered up the dead which were in them: and they were judged every man according

<u>**to their works.**</u>

Judgment will be meted out based upon works. Some sins are far worse than others. Punishment will be determined based upon "those things which were written in the books, according to their works" (v. 12).

After "the Great White Throne Judgment," righteous has been restored. There will no longer be a need for death and hades. Death was the penalty for sin beginning with Adam. Hades was the holding place for those who had sinned and were awaiting judgment. Verses 14-15:

> 14 **And death and hell [hades] were cast into the lake of fire. This is the second death.** 15 **And whosoever was not found written in the book of life was cast into the lake of fire.**

This is part of the restoration process in which G-d will complete His purpose. Judgment must be part of the restoration of fallen Creation. The eternal Kingdom will be ruled by its righteous King.

The last item on Daniel's list is the anointing of the Most Holy. This formality remains to be completed. We all know the King will be Yeshua HaMashiach – the Righteous One. For no one else is worthy. He is a descendent of King David. He is the Son of David and the Son of Man through His earthly mother. He is also the Son of G-d. He is the One Who will be anointed to rule over Creation.

In Revelation, John describes the new heaven and new earth in verses 21.1-2:

> 1 And I saw a new heaven and a new earth: for the first heaven and the first earth were passed away; and there was no more sea.

> 2 And I John saw the holy city, new Jerusalem, coming down from G-d out of heaven, prepared as a bride adorned for her husband.

All of us have seen a radiant bride walking down the aisle to meet her beloved. John describes this glorious Holy City – Jerusalem. Verses 3-4:

> 3 And I heard a great voice out of heaven saying, Behold, the tabernacle of G-d is with men, and he will dwell with them, and they shall be his people, and G-d himself shall be with them, and be their G-d.

> 4 And G-d shall wipe away all tears

from their eyes; and there shall be no more death, neither sorrow, nor crying, neither shall there be any more pain: for the former things are passed away.

Everything will be new! There will be no more sorrow, tears, death, crying, or pain for it will all be removed. It would be impossible to experience those things while living in the presence of the Righteous King – the Creator of the Universe.

John continues with his description of the King Himself in verses 5-6:

5 And he [HaMashiach] that sat upon the throne said, Behold, I make all things new. And he [HaMashiach] said unto me [John], Write: for these words are true and faithful.

6 And he [HaMashiach] said unto me [John], It is done [complete]. I am Alpha and Omega, the beginning and the end. I will give unto him that is athirst [thirsty] of the fountain of the water of life [to drink] freely.

HaMashiach speaks directly to those who *overcame* in verse 7. From this, it is clear He is speaking to Israel – those who believed, kept their faith with their actions as proof, and endured unto the end. They fulfilled the requirements according to the Kingdom Gospel. Verses 7-8:

> 7 **He that overcometh shall inherit all things; and I will be his G-d, and he shall be my son.**

> 8 **But the fearful, and unbelieving, and the abominable, and murderers, and whoremongers, and sorcerers, and idolaters, and all liars, shall [continue to] have their part in the lake which burneth with fire and brimstone: which is the second death.**

The judgments are over. It was necessary for them to be completed prior to the arrival of the Bride who will appear in her glorious radiance – the New Jerusalem!

29

The Eternal Shabbat

The Hebrew word "Shabbat" is derived from the root "Shavat" meaning "to cease" or "to rest." G-d created the heaven and the earth in six days and then, on the seventh day, He rested. We have arrived at the final day in the restoration. It is the completion of G-d's plan to restore His Creation. It is important that all the work be completed before the Sabbath. In Creation, it was on the Sabbath that G-d not only rested, but saw that all was good.

You may remember the declaration by John the Baptist when he saw Yeshua approaching him. John 1.29:

> 29 The next day John [the Baptist] seeth [Yeshua] coming unto him, and saith, <u>Behold the Lamb of G-d, which taketh away the sin of the world.</u>

John the Baptist called Yeshua "the Lamb of G-d" referring to the Passover Lamb. In the book of Revelation, the title "the Lamb" will be used eight times. Each time it directly refers to Yeshua HaMashiach. For G-d Himself had provided the sacrifice in the same way that He saved Isaac. His sacrifice is sufficient to meet all the requirements of the Law.

The Seventh Day

The Apostle John inspires our imaginations as he describes the eternal City of G-d – the Bride. An angel or messenger invited John to come and see the Bride of the Lamb. The New Jerusalem is beautifully described in great detail. The following lists the number of memorials G-d made to the individual tribes of Israel. This is the glorious destiny of Israel. Verses 9-16:

> 9 **And there came unto me one of the seven angels which had the seven vials full of the seven last plagues, and talked with me, saying, Come hither [here], <u>I will shew thee the bride, the Lamb's wife.</u>**
>
> 10 **And he carried me away in the spirit to a great and high mountain, and shewed me <u>that great city, the holy Jerusalem</u>, descending out of heaven**

from G-d, 11 Having the glory of G-d: and her light was like unto a stone most precious, even like a jasper stone, clear as crystal;

12 And had a wall great and high, and had <u>twelve gates</u>, and at the gates twelve angels, and names written thereon, which are <u>the names of the twelve tribes of the children of Israel</u>: 13 On the east three gates; on the north three gates; on the south three gates; and on the west three gates. 14 <u>And the wall of the city had twelve foundations, and in them the names of the twelve apostles of the Lamb.</u>

15 And he that talked with me had a golden reed to measure the city, and the gates thereof, and the wall thereof. 16 And the city lieth foursquare, and the length is as large as the breadth: and he measured the city with the reed, twelve thousand furlongs. The length and the breadth and the height of it are equal.

The New Jerusalem was measured by the angel. A cubit is a measurement determined by the distance between a man's elbow to the end of his longest finger. John corrects himself. He informs his reader that it was not a man's cubit, but an angel's cubit that determined the measurements. Verses 17-21:

> 17 And he measured the wall thereof, an hundred and forty and four cubits, <u>according to the measure of a man, that is, of the angel</u>. 18 And the building of the wall of it was of jasper: and the city was pure gold, like unto clear glass.

> 19 And the foundations of the wall of the city were garnished with all manner of precious stones. The first foundation was jasper; the second, sapphire; the third, a chalcedony; the fourth, an emerald; 20 The fifth, sardonyx; the sixth, sardius; the seventh, chrysolite; the eighth, beryl; the ninth, a topaz; the tenth, a chrysoprasus; the eleventh, a jacinth; the twelfth, an amethyst.

> 21 And the twelve gates were twelve pearls; every several [separate] gate was of one pearl: and the street of the city was pure gold, as it were transparent glass.

The word "tabernacle" can be both a noun,

meaning "a meeting place," or a verb meaning "to dwell with." For Israel, this has great significance. The original "tabernacle" was constructed by their forefathers in the Wilderness. It was both a temporary meeting place and a dwelling place for G-d. Now, we are told that G-d will dwell with His people Israel . . . forever! Verses 22-23:

> 22 And I saw no temple therein: for the Lord G-d Almighty and the Lamb are [Themselves] the temple of it. 23 And the city had no need of the sun, neither of the moon, to shine in it: for the glory of G-d did lighten it, and the Lamb is the light thereof.

There will be Gentile nations in the future. They will bring their *glory and honor* which is their praise and offering to G-d. Verses 24-25:

> 24 And the nations of them which are saved shall walk in the light of it: and the kings of the earth do bring their glory and honour into it. 25 And the gates of it shall not be shut at all by day: for there shall be no night there.

The nation of Israel was created by G-d with a unique purpose. We find this spoken of in the book of Exodus. G-d is speaking to Israel through Moses in verses 19.5-6:

> 5 Now therefore, if ye will hearken unto My voice indeed, and keep My covenant, then <u>ye shall be Mine own treasure</u> from among all peoples; for all the earth is Mine; 6 and <u>ye shall be unto Me a kingdom of priests</u>, and a holy nation. These are the words which thou shalt speak unto the children of Israel.'

G-d has always intended Israel to be "a kingdom of priests." The purpose of a priest is to act as an intermediary between G-d and someone else. Israel would intercede for the Nations on G-d's behalf.

Zechariah was a prophet in the 6th century BCE. That was over six hundred years before the birth of Yeshua. Notice the nations making pilgrimages to Jerusalem to seek G-d's favor. Zechariah 8.20-23:

> 20 Thus saith the LORD of hosts: It shall yet come to pass, that there shall come peoples, and the inhabitants of many cities; 21 and the inhabitants of one city shall go to another, saying: Let us go speedily to entreat the favour of the LORD, and to seek the LORD of

hosts; I will go also.

22 Yea, many peoples and mighty nations shall come to seek the LORD of hosts in Jerusalem, and to entreat the favour of the LORD.

23 Thus saith the LORD of hosts: In those days it shall come to pass, that ten men shall take hold, out of all the languages of the nations, shall even take hold of the skirt of him that is a Jew, saying: We will go with you, for we have heard that G-d is with you.

The Gentiles will seek the Jews who have a special relationship with G-d. Therefore, it will be the Jews' unique purpose to approach G-d on behalf of these nations. They will act as intermediaries for the nations. In the new Creation, HaMashiach will be with G-d and dwell in the New Jerusalem. The Nations will come but they can only approach G-d through His priests – the nation of Israel!

The text speaks of nations and Gentile kings. However, nothing that defiles will be allowed to enter. Revelation 21.26-27:

26 And they [the nations and the kings of the earth] shall bring the glory and

honour of the nations into it [the eternal city]. 27 And there shall in no wise [way] enter into it any thing that defileth, neither whatsoever worketh abomination, or maketh a lie: but they which are written in the Lamb's book of life.

Much like the water that flowed from the Rock in the wilderness, so will the source of water be found coming out of the New Jerusalem. Revelation 22.1:

1 And he shewed me a pure river of water of life, clear as crystal, proceeding out of the throne of G-d and of the Lamb.

A river will flow out of the throne of both G-d and the Lamb. The finished restoration of G-d's Creation will have a connection with the Garden of Eden. In the same way that a river will flow and envelope an island, there we will find the Tree of Life. In Genesis 3, G-d expelled Adam and Eve from the Garden of Eden to prevent them from eating from the Tree of Life. Here we find this same Tree of Life planted in the New Jerusalem! Verses 2-5:

2 In the midst of the street of it, and on either side of the river, was there the

tree of life, which bare twelve manner [types] of fruits, and yielded her fruit every month: and the leaves of the tree were for the healing of the nations. 3 And there shall be no more curse: but the throne of G-d and of the Lamb shall be in it; and his servants shall serve him:

4 And they shall see his face; and his name shall be in their foreheads. 5 And there shall be no night there; and they need no candle, neither light of the sun; for the Lord G-d giveth them light: and they shall reign for ever and ever.

There will be no night; no need for the sun or the moon. G-d will provide the Light. From the New Jerusalem, G-d and the Lamb reign forever. That brings us to the last item on Daniel's checklist: the anointing of the Most Holy.

G-d tells the Apostle John everything which he was told is true and these events will happen shortly. Revelation is a book of prophecy. It is also the final book of truth which reveals Yeshua Ha-Mashiach. John is told that those who keep or hold these truths of this book in their heart will be blessed. Why? They will understanding what is happening and planned by G-d. Verses 6-7:

> 6 And he said unto me, These sayings
> are faithful and true: and the Lord G-d
> of the holy prophets sent his angel to
> shew unto his servants the things
> which must shortly be done.

> 7 Behold, I come quickly: blessed is he
> that keepeth the sayings of the prophe-
> cy of this book.

All this is overwhelming for John and he falls at the
feet of the angel, or messenger. He began to give the
angel words of praise, but the angel stopped him.
He reminded him only G-d is worthy to be worshipped. Verses 8-9:

> 8 And I John saw these things, and
> heard them. And when I had heard and
> seen, I fell down to worship before the
> feet of the angel which shewed me
> these things.

> 9 Then saith he [the angel] unto me,
> See thou do it not: for I am thy fel-
> lowservant, and of thy brethren the
> prophets, and of them which keep the
> sayings of this book: worship G-d.

The angel claims to be much like John, a fellow servant of the Most High. Then, much like Gabriel instructed Daniel, the angel instructed John. John is told that what he has learned should not be hidden because these events are imminent. He is to let or allow others to continue to be as they are. In other words, let people be and do not try to change them. They are what they are and there is little time left. John's vision occurred in the late first century sometime prior to his death in circa 90 CE. Verses 10-11:

> 10 **And he saith unto me, Seal not [Do not hide] the sayings of the prophecy of this book: for the time is at hand.** 11 **He that is unjust, let him be unjust still: and he which is filthy, let him be filthy still: and he that is righteous, let him be righteous still: and he that is holy, let him be holy still.**

John was part of the Age of Law. For the Jews, it was always about the Kingdom and their eternal King Who will rule over the earth. It has always been about Israel and the Gentile nations who will surround that Kingdom.

It is a King's prerogative or right to reward those whom He chooses. There are those in the Kingdom who will receive rewards according to their works. The rewards are His alone to give. Verses 12-13:

> 12 **And, behold, I come quickly; and <u>my reward is with me, to give every man according as his work shall be</u>.** 13 **I am Alpha and Omega, the beginning and the end, the first and the last.**

Those faithful and obedient to the Law will have access to the Tree of Life. They may freely enter the enteral city through its gates. The New Jerusalem will be free from corruption. Verses 14-15:

> 14 **Blessed are they that do his commandments [follow His Laws], that they may have right to the tree of life, and may enter in through the gates into the city.**

> 15 **For without [outside] are dogs, and sorcerers, and whoremongers, and murderers, and idolaters, and whosoever loveth and maketh a lie.**

Yeshua declared to John that He is the rightful heir to the throne of David, King of Israel. This is important for both Israel and the Gentiles to hear this. For Yeshua HaMashiach, Who is the Creator (*cf.* Colossians 1.16-17). He calls Himself "the root" or father of David. Yet, as Mary's son and a direct descendant of King David, He calls Himself "the offspring" or the Son of David. As G-d, He would be both. Verse 16:

> 16 I [Yeshua] have sent mine angel [messenger] to testify unto you these things in the churches. I am <u>the root and the offspring of David</u>, and the bright and morning star.

The Apostle Paul gave an excellent allegory to the Gentiles as we taught them about the New Jerusalem. Galatians 4.22-23:

> 22 For it is written, that Abraham had two sons, the one by a bondmaid, the other by a freewoman.

> 23 But he who was of the bondwoman was born after the flesh; but he of the freewoman was by promise.

In Genesis, Hagar was Sarah's handmaid. Sarah was unable to produce a child on her own to fulfill G-d's promise to Abraham. So, she had Abraham sleep with her maid to obtain an heir. Hagar conceived a son and he was named Ishmael. However, according to the promise, G-d Himself provided an heir by causing Sarah to conceive in her late in years. She bore Abraham a son named Isaac. Paul continues with his explanation in verses 24-26:

> 24 Which things are an allegory: for these are the two covenants; the one from the mount Sinai, which gendereth [gave birth] to bondage, which is Agar. 25 For this Agar is mount Sinai in Arabia, and answereth to Jerusalem which now is [old Jerusalem], and is in bondage with her children.
>
> 26 But [the New] Jerusalem which is [from] above is free, which is the mother of us all.

The New Jerusalem from above will be free; no longer in bondage to sin. This is the fulfillment of G-d's "unconditional promises" made to Abraham and David. For this reason, the New Jerusalem, which is from above, will figuratively become the Bride of HaMashiach. Revelation 22.17:

> 17 And the Spirit and the bride say, Come. And let him that heareth say, Come. And let him that is athirst come. And whosoever will [chooses], let him take the water of life freely.

The book of Revelation completes the revelation of

G-d to man. As comes to the end, it does so with a stern warning to those who may alter it. There is a curse placed upon anyone who adds or removes words from this book. Verses 18-19:

> 18 For I testify unto every man that heareth the words of the prophecy of this book, If any man shall add unto these things, G-d shall add unto him the plagues that are written in this book:

> 19 And if any man shall take away from the words of the book of this prophecy, G-d shall take away his part out of the book of life, and out of the holy city, and from the things which are written in this book.

The Apostle John ends the book by quoting the Word of G-d in verse 20:

> 20 He [HaMashiach] which testifieth [of] these things saith, Surely I [HaMashiach] come quickly. Amen. Even so, come, Lord [Yeshua].

John end with this benediction. Verse 21:

> 21 The grace of our Lord [Yeshua Ha-

Mashiach] be with you all. Amen.

30

Putting The Pieces Together

Finally, we have come to the end. I would like to thank you for staying with me. When we stop and think about Scripture, it may feel like the puzzle pieces in a box. The purpose of this book was to provide you with a framework in which you can see Scripture as a whole. Most puzzles come in boxes with a picture of the completed picture on the cover. We looked at only the highlights in order to gain an overall understanding of Scripture. Understanding its structure or framework, can help anyone who wants to know G-d and His plan. Scripture is closed revelation which means it has been sealed. Nothing can be added to or subtracted from what G-d has revealed in His Word. In other words, from Genesis to Revelation, G-d's revelation is complete.

There is only one G-d. Think about Melchisedec, the king of Salem, who accepted worship from Abraham and also accepted a tenth of his spoils as an offering or gift. Hebrews 7.1-3:

> 1 **For this Melchisedec, king of Salem, priest of the most high G-d, who met Abraham returning from the slaughter of the kings, and blessed him;**
>
> 2 **To whom also Abraham gave a tenth part of all; first <u>being by interpretation King of righteousness, and after that also King of Salem, which is, King of peace;</u>** 3 <u>**Without father, without mother, without descent, having neither beginning of days, nor end of life; but made like unto the Son of G-d; abideth a priest continually.**</u>

Presently, this same High Priest serves in the heavenly tabernacle daily interceding on Israel's behalf before G-d.

In Chapter 7, we explored how Jacob's name was changed to Israel. Was it not G-d Who, in human form, wrestled with our forefather Jacob? G-d placed Moses in the cleft of the rock and passed by so that Moses could see His backside; for no one could see the face of G-d and live. In the book of Revelation, we see Yeshua HaMashiach is anointed as the King Eternal. He will destroy the nations who are Israel's enemies just like He did with Pharaoh and his army. All of these stories you can read and consider in your independent study. Each of these can be placed within the framework of the Seven Days.

HaMashiach has always had a unique relationship with Israel. This relationship will continue for eternity. They are His brethren. He was born of a Hebrew woman and the legitimate heir to David's throne. David was a shepherd-king and, like him, Yeshua will also shepherd His people Israel. Look at the following words spoken by Yeshua. John 10.11-15:

> 11 <u>I am the good shepherd</u>: the good shepherd giveth his life for the sheep. 12 But he that is an hireling, and not the shepherd, whose own the sheep are not, seeth the wolf coming, and leaveth the sheep, and fleeth: and the wolf catcheth them, and scattereth the sheep.
>
> 13 The hireling fleeth, because he is an hireling, and careth not for the sheep. 14 <u>I am the good shepherd, and know my sheep, and am known of [by] mine</u>.
>
> 15 As the Father knoweth me, even so know I the Father: and <u>I lay down my</u>

life for the sheep.

Yeshua's earthly ministry was exclusively to Israel. The Apostle Paul stated, "Now I say that [Yeshua HaMashiach] was a minister of the circumcision for the truth of G-d, to confirm the promises made unto the fathers" (Rom. 15:8). As such, He directed His Twelve specifically to bring the Gospel of the Kingdom to Israel. Matthew 10:5-7:

> 5 **These twelve Jesus sent forth, and commanded them, saying, Go not into the way of the Gentiles, and into any city of the Samaritans enter ye not:**
>
> 6 **But go rather to the lost sheep of the house of Israel. 7 And as ye go, preach, saying, The kingdom of heaven is at hand.**

This message and its intended recipients never changed! This same message applies to Israel today until G-d completes His plans for them. There are many other stories in the Bible that prove Yeshua HaMashiach was, is, and will be The Great Shepherd of Israel.

Therefore, when the wolf is seen coming, do not be afraid! Towards the end of the seven years, Israel will be surrounded by wolves. The nations will seek to destroy G-d's people. Yet, the mighty Shepherd-King will come again to defend and destroy these wolves. Those who endure and keep their faith in the Word of the LORD unto the end will be saved. At the great battle, we read the record of His Coming — The King Victorious. At His appearance the Israel's enemies will melt like wax before the Son. Revelation 19.11-13:

> 11 **And I saw heaven opened, and behold a white horse; and he that sat upon him was called Faithful and True, and in righteousness he doth judge and make war.**
>
> 12 **His eyes were as a flame of fire, and on his head were many crowns; and he had a name written, that no man knew, but he himself.**
>
> 13 **And he was clothed with a vesture dipped in blood: and his name is called <u>The Word of G-d</u>.**

Throughout this book we have referred to the inspired Scripture as G-d's Word. His Word is perfect. G-d entrusted to the Jews the oracles of G-d! (*cf.* Rom. 3.1-2.)

Yeshua HaMashiach is speaking in Revelation

22.12-13:

> 12 **And, behold, I come quickly; and my reward is with me, to give every man according as his work shall be.**
>
> 13 <u>**I am Alpha and Omega, the beginning and the end, the first and the last**</u>.

He is the Alpha and Omega which represent the beginning and the end. The One Who walked in the Garden of Eden in the cool of the day will return to claim His throne as the Eternal King.

The Apostle Paul taught the Gentiles to understand Israel. He made an interesting point concerning the seed of Abraham. Galatians 3.15-18:

> 15 **Brethren, I speak after the manner of men; Though it be but a man's covenant, yet if it be confirmed, no man disannulleth, or addeth thereto.**
>
> 16 **Now to Abraham and his seed were the promises made. He saith not, And to seeds, as of many; but as of one, And to thy seed, which is [HaMashiach].**
>
> 17 **And this I say, that the covenant, that was confirmed before of G-d in [Ha-**

Mashiach], the law, which was four hundred and thirty years after, cannot disannul, that it should make the promise of none effect.

18 <u>For if the inheritance be of the law, it is no more of promise: but G-d gave it to Abraham by promise</u>.

Paul was saying that the promise G-d made to Abraham was to made to Abraham and his Seed. That Seed was singular. That Seed is HaMashiach. He did not say to Abraham and his seeds which are all his descendants. His second point is this. If the inheritance promised to Abraham was by the Law, then "it would be earned by keeping the Law" and, therefore, "it would no longer be a gift by promise." G-d gave it to Abraham as "a *gift*." This means that the promise was "given" and not be "earned."

Peter, the Apostle to the Circumcision, found it difficult to understand Paul. Peter mentioned this as he wrote to the Jews. 2 Peter 3.13-16:

13 Nevertheless we, according to his promise, look for new heavens and a new earth, wherein dwelleth right- eousness. 14 Wherefore, beloved, see- ing that ye look for such things, be dil- igent that ye may be found of him in

peace, without spot, and blameless.

15 And account that the longsuffering of our Lord is salvation; even as our beloved brother Paul also according to the wisdom given unto him hath written unto you;

16 As also in all his epistles, speaking in them of these things; in which are some things hard to be understood, which they that are unlearned and unstable wrest, as they do also the other scriptures, unto their own destruction.

The book of Revelation reveals the completion of G-d's plan to restore Creation. There is the revelation of Yeshua HaMashiach as the Lamb of G-d who takes away the sins of the world. He is the G-od's. He is HaMashiach and the Eternal King of Israel.

These final verses in Revelation seal up Scripture. After you read these verses, read them a second time, but use the word "gift" instead of the word "grace." It sums up G-d's purpose. Verses 20-21:

20 He [Yeshua] which testifieth these things saith, Surely I come quickly. Amen. Even so, come, Lord [Yeshua].

21 The grace of our Lord [Yeshua Ha-Mashiach] be with you all. Amen.

Other GraceWord Publications

337

El Evangelio Oculto: Una vez fue un misterio . . .
Efesios: Dispensacionalmente considerado

Letters To Theophilus provides a deeper understanding of three systems used to interpret Scripture. These systems are explained. Each is then tested using a "test of truth" which requires a successful system to be applied to the entire Bible with no failures. This book is the "other side of the coin." Whereas *The Glorious Destiny of Israel* applies to the Jews, *Letters To Theophilus* presents Paul's Gospel of Grace sent to the Gentiles. Both of these books apply the dispensational tool in their interpretation.

About The Author

Dr. David Alan Greene has over thirty-five years of experience as an insurance agent selling both property and casualty as well as life insurance. During his career, he taught and explained the content and meaning of policies to his clients. Now retired, he devotes much of his time to teaching the Bible.

He obtained his Bachelor of Theology, Master of Biblical Studies, and Ph.D. in Biblical Studies from Evangelical Theological Seminary where he holds the position of Dean of Graduate Studies. He also holds a Ph.D. in Christian Counseling. He has written numerous biblical commentaries and books on rightly dividing the Word of Truth.

ww.ingramcontent.com/pod-product-compliance
htning Source LLC
bersburg PA
060758120626
CB00001B/15